INDIANA
Language Arts Test Preparation Workbook

Third Course

HOLT, RINEHART AND WINSTON
A Harcourt Education Company

Orlando • **Austin** • New York • San Diego • London

Copyright © by Holt, Rinehart and Winston

All rights reserved. No part of this publication may be reproduced or transmitted in any form or by any means, electronic or mechanical, including photocopy, recording, or any information storage and retrieval system, without permission in writing from the publisher.

Teachers using **ELEMENTS OF LITERATURE** or **ELEMENTS OF LANGUAGE** may photocopy complete pages in sufficient quantities for classroom use only and not for resale.

Indiana Teacher Contributors/Reviewers

Jillian Allyn
Castle High School
Newburgh, Indiana

Candace Maicher
Morton High School
Hammond, Indiana

Rick Reed
Warren Central High School
Indianapolis, Indiana

Nicole Conder
Castle High School
Newburgh, Indiana

Pamela Mason
Scribner Middle School
New Albany, Indiana

Kristine M. Rentsch
Castle High School
Newburgh, Indiana

Deborah C. Cuffia
Crown Point High School
Crown Point, Indiana

Rebecca McGuckin
Clay Middle School
Carmel, Indiana

Bob Roach
Franklin Township Middle School
Indianapolis, Indiana

Beth Ann Euler
Castle High School
Newburgh, Indiana

Donna Middleton
Thompkins Middle School
Evansville, Indiana

Kevin Sandorf
Howe Academy
Indianapolis, Indiana

Cynthia Ewick
Perry Meridian Middle School
Indianapolis, Indiana

Maggie Nuttall
Franklin Township Middle School
Indianapolis, Indiana

Bonnie Shipman
Huntington North High School
Huntington, Indiana

A. M. Hammons
Wm. H. Harrison High School
West Lafayette, Indiana

Gayle L. Pannell
Franklin Township Middle School
Indianapolis, Indiana

Jennifer Jacobs
Hamilton Southeastern High School
Fishers, Indiana

Luann Reabe
Kitley Intermediate School
Indianapolis, Indiana

ELEMENTS OF LANGUAGE, ELEMENTS OF LITERATURE, HOLT, and the **"Owl Design"** are trademarks licensed to Holt, Rinehart and Winston, registered in the United States of America and/or other jurisdictions.

Printed in the United States of America

If you have received these materials as examination copies free of charge, Holt, Rinehart and Winston retains title to the materials and they may not be resold. Resale of examination copies is strictly prohibited.

Possession of this publication in print format does not entitle users to convert this publication, or any portion of it, into electronic format.

ISBN-13 978-0-03-079193-2

ISBN-10   0-03-079193-6

2 3 4 5 179 09 08

TABLE OF CONTENTS

To the Student iv

Tracking Your Progress v

Test Tips for Students 1

Reading Test Practice 5
   Introduction 6
   Reading Selections with Questions 12–64

Writing Test Practice 65
   Introduction 66
   Graphic Organizers for Writing 71
   Writing Prompts 74–109
   Writing Conventions Practice 110–122

Indiana Grade 9 Practice Test 123–162

Answer Sheets 163

TO THE STUDENT

This booklet provides you with reading and writing test practice as well as one Indiana practice test. We have also included a Mastery Grid, which will help you chart your progress as you work to master the Indiana Standards.

This test preparation booklet also includes tips on answering the types of questions you'll see on the *ISTEP+*, *ISTEP+* GQE in reading and writing. There are suggestions for answering multiple-choice and open-ended questions and for responding to writing prompts.

Name _____

TRACKING YOUR PROGRESS

Indiana Reading and Writing

Grade 9 Objective	Grade 8 Objective	Test Item	Page Number	Mastery Yes	Mastery No	Date	Comments/ Questions
9.1.1	8.1.3	4	23				
	8.1.1	1	36				
		5	40				
	8.1.3	4	47				
		10	49				
	8.1.1	7	57				
		8	57				
9.1.1; 9.1.2		12	130				
9.1.2		7	45				
	8.1.3	8	53				
	8.3.4; 8.3.9	3	126				
		4	127				
9.1.2; 9.2.7		5	34				
9.2.1		4	33				
	8.2.7	9	34				
		2	47				
	8.2.5	3	52				
	8.2.1	7	53				
	8.2.6	19	133				
	8.2.1	24	137				
9.2.1; 9.2.7	8.2.9	5	57				
9.2.3	8.2.9	8	40				
		8	60				
	8.2.9	18	133				
	8.2.7	25	137				
9.2.4	8.2.3	7	48				
9.2.4; 9.2.7; 9.2.8	8.2.2; 8.2.9	9	45				
9.2.6	8.2.4	1	52				
	8.2.6	9	57				
	8.2.9	20	133				
	8.2.6	22	137				
9.2.6; 9.2.7	8.2.6; 8.2.7	9	49				
		10	57				
	8.2.6	10	61				
9.2.6; 9.2.8	8.2.6; 8.2.7	6	48				

Copyright © by Holt, Rinehart and Winston. All rights reserved.

v

Name

TRACKING YOUR PROGRESS

Indiana Reading and Writing

Grade 9 Objective	Grade 8 Objective	Test Item	Page Number	Mastery Yes	Mastery No	Date	Comments/ Questions
9.2.6; 9.2.8	8.2.9	7	60				
9.2.7	8.2.9	5	13				
	8.2.7	1	39				
	8.2.6; 8.2.7	3	44				
	8.2.7	4	44				
	8.2.5	8	48				
	8.2.7	6	53				
	8.2.6	10	53				
	8.2.5	2	56				
		1	59				
	8.2.6; 8.2.7	9	61				
		23	137				
	8.2.7	27	138				
9.2.7; 9.2.8	8.2.2; 8.2.5; 8.2.9	10	45				
	8.2.9	4	56				
		6	57				
	8.2.7	1	44				
	8.2.9	5	52				
9.2.8		1	13				
	8.2.4	1	33				
	8.2.9	8	34				
		3	39				
	8.2.6	4	39				
	8.2.4	9	40				
	8.2.9	5	44				
		6	45				
		8	45				
	8.2.5	1	47				
	8.2.9	3	47				
		4	52				
	8.2.9	6	60				
		15	132				
	8.2.5	21	134				
9.3.11	8.3.6	9	25				
	8.1.3	6	37				

Copyright © by Holt, Rinehart and Winston. All rights reserved.

Name

TRACKING YOUR PROGRESS

Indiana Reading and Writing

Grade 9 Objective	Grade 8 Objective	Test Item	Page Number	Mastery Yes	Mastery No	Date	Comments/ Questions
9.3.11		3	63				
	8.3.6	30	141				
9.3.12	8.3.3	10	14				
	8.3.7; 8.3.9	8	37				
	8.3.5	32	142				
	8.3.7	33	142				
9.3.13	8.3.8	10	37				
		11	129				
9.3.2		2	13				
		8	64				
9.3.3	8.3.2	6	18				
		10	19				
9.3.3; 9.3.8	8.3.3	2	28				
9.3.4	8.3.3	6	14				
		1	17				
		4	17				
		5	18				
		1	23				
	8.3.3	5	24				
		9	30				
		1	126				
		6	127				
		34	142				
9.3.4; 9.2.8	8.3.3	7	14				
9.3.5	8.3.5	8	18				
	8.3.7	5	29				
	8.3.5	7	37				
		10	64				
9.3.6	8.2.7	3	13				
		4	13				
	8.3.6	3	17				
	8.3.2	31	142				
9.3.7	8.3.6	2	17				
		2	23				
		1	28				
	8.1.1	4	28				

Copyright © by Holt, Rinehart and Winston. All rights reserved.

vii

Name _____

TRACKING YOUR PROGRESS

Indiana Reading and Writing

Grade 9 Objective	Grade 8 Objective	Test Item	Page Number	Mastery Yes	Mastery No	Date	Comments/ Questions
9.3.7	8.1.1	3	36				
	8.3.6	5	37				
		2	63				
		4	63				
	8.1.1; 8.3.6	9	64				
		9	129				
	8.3.6	10	129				
9.3.7; 9.3.11	8.3.6	7	29				
	8.1.1	2	36				
9.3.7; 9.3.9	8.3.4; 8.3.9	6	24				
9.3.8	8.3.2	10	25				
	8.3.6	3	28				
	8.3.7	10	30				
	8.3.3	2	126				
	8.3.6	7	127				
9.3.9	8.3.8	7	24				
9.3.9; 9.3.13	8.3.8	8	129				
9.4.1	8.4.1	4	59				
9.4.12	8.4.7	3	56				
		2	59				
9.5.4	8.2.6	3	59				
	8.1.3	8	14				
		9	14				
		7	18				
	8.1.1	9	19				
	8.1.1; 8.3.6	3	23				
	8.3.6	8	24				
	8.1.3	6	29				
	8.3.2	8	30				
	8.2.7	2	33				
	8.2.4	3	33				
	8.1.3	6	34				
	8.2.4	7	34				
	8.2.5	10	34				
	8.3.4; 8.3.9	4	36				

Copyright © by Holt, Rinehart and Winston. All rights reserved.

Name _____

TRACKING YOUR PROGRESS

Indiana Reading and Writing

Grade 9 Objective	Grade 8 Objective	Test Item	Page Number	Mastery Yes	Mastery No	Date	Comments/ Questions
	8.3.1	9	37				
	8.2.5	2	39				
	8.1.3	6	40				
	8.2.5	7	40				
	8.2.7	10	41				
	8.2.6; 8.2.7; 8.2.9	2	44				
	8.2.4	5	48				
	8.2.5	2	52				
	8.2.4	9	53				
	8.1.3	1	56				
	8.4.10	5	60				
	8.3.4; 8.3.9	1	63				
	8.3.1	5	63				
	8.1.1; 8.3.6	6	63				
	8.3.8	7	64				
	8.1.3	5	127				
	8.3.1	13	130				
	8.3.7	14	130				
	8.1.3	16	132				
	8.2.4	17	132				
	8.2.3; 8.2.7	26	138				
	8.1.3	28	141				
	8.3.2	29	141				
9.4.2; 9.4.3; 9.4.5; 9.4.10; 9.4.11; 9.4.12; 9.4.13; 9.5.1; 9.5.7; 9.5.8; 9.6.1; 9.6.2; 9.6.3; 9.6.4	8.4.1; 8.4.2; 8.4.3; 8.4.7; 8.4.8; 8.4.9; 8.4.10; 8.5.1; 8.5.6; 8.5.7; 8.6.1; 8.6.2; 8.6.3; 8.6.4; 8.6.5; 8.6.6; 8.6.7	WP	149				
9.4.10	8.6.5	56	153				
	8.6.2	57	154				
	8.6.7	58	154				

Copyright © by Holt, Rinehart and Winston. All rights reserved.

ix

Name

TRACKING YOUR PROGRESS

Indiana Reading and Writing

Grade 9 Objective	Grade 8 Objective	Test Item	Page Number	Mastery Yes	Mastery No	Date	Comments/ Questions
9.4.10	8.4.7	62	156				
	8.6.4	64	156				
		65	157				
		68	158				
	8.4.7; 8.6.7	7	120				
	8.6.3	8	120				
	8.4.9	9	120				
	8.6.4	12	121				
9.4.12	8.4.9	52	152				
		53	152				
		54	153				
		69	158				
		71	159				
		14	122				
		15	122				
9.4.13	8.4.9	60	155				
		66	157				
		73	160				
9.4.2	8.4.9	61	155				
		13	122				
9.4.2; 9.4.3; 9.4.10; 9.4.11; 9.4.12; 9.4.13; 9.5.1; 9.5.7; 9.5.8; 9.6.1; 9.6.2; 9.6.3; 9.6.4	8.4.1; 8.4.2; 8.4.3; 8.4.7; 8.4.8; 8.4.9; 8.4.10; 8.5.2; 8.5.6; 8.5.7; 8.6.1; 8.6.2; 8.6.3; 8.6.4; 8.6.5; 8.6.6; 8.6.7	WP2	83				
9.4.2; 9.4.3; 9.4.10; 9.4.11; 9.4.12; 9.4.13; 9.5.3; 9.5.7; 9.5.8; 9.6.1; 9.6.2; 9.6.3; 9.6.4	8.4.1; 8.4.2; 8.4.3; 8.4.7; 8.4.8; 8.4.9; 8.4.10; 8.5.6; 8.5.7; 8.6.1; 8.6.2; 8.6.3; 8.6.4; 8.6.5; 8.6.6; 8.6.7	WP4	101				

Copyright © by Holt, Rinehart and Winston. All rights reserved.

Name _____

TRACKING YOUR PROGRESS

Indiana Writing

Grade 9 Objective	Grade 8 Objective	Test Item	Page Number	Mastery Yes	Mastery No	Date	Comments/ Questions
9.4.2; 9.4.3; 9.4.5; 9.4.10; 9.4.11; 9.4.12; 9.4.13; 9.5.4; 9.5.7; 9.5.8; 9.6.1; 9.6.2; 9.6.3; 9.6.4	8.4.1; 8.4.2; 8.4.3; 8.4.7; 8.4.8; 8.4.9; 8.4.10; 8.5.4; 8.5.6; 8.5.7; 8.6.1; 8.6.2; 8.6.3; 8.6.4; 8.6.5; 8.6.6; 8.6.7	WP1	74				
9.4.2; 9.4.3; 9.4.5; 9.4.7; 9.4.10; 9.4.11; 9.4.12; 9.4.13; 9.5.3; 9.5.7; 9.5.8; 9.6.1; 9.6.2; 9.6.3; 9.6.4	8.4.1; 8.4.2; 8.4.3; 8.4.5; 8.4.7; 8.4.8; 8.4.9; 8.4.10; 8.5.6; 8.5.7; 8.6.1; 8.6.2; 8.6.3; 8.6.4; 8.6.5; 8.6.5; 8.6.6; 8.6.7	WP3	92				
9.4.3	8.4.9	70	159				
		6	119				
9.5.8		72	160				
9.6.1	8.6.4	40	147				
		42	147				
	8.6.1	67	157				
	8.6.4	5	113				
	8.6.1	6	113				
	8.6.5	2	115				
	8.6.1; 8.6.3	5	115				
	8.6.3	6	117				
	8.6.4	3	118				
	8.6.1	11	121				
9.6.1; 9.6.3	8.6.5	3	115				
9.6.2	8.6.4	37	144				
		39	145				
		43	147				
		44	148				
	8.6.5	47	150				
	8.6.4	49	151				

Name

TRACKING YOUR PROGRESS

Indiana Writing

Grade 9 Objective	Grade 8 Objective	Test Item	Page Number	Mastery Yes	Mastery No	Date	Comments/ Questions
9.6.2	8.6.4	50	151				
		55	153				
		63	156				
	8.6.3; 8.6.4	6	111				
	8.6.3	1	113				
	8.6.4	2	113				
		6	115				
		2	117				
	8.6.1; 8.6.5	4	117				
	8.6.4	2	118				
		10	121				
9.6.3	8.6.7	35	144				
	8.6.6	36	144				
	8.6.5	38	144				
	8.6.7	41	147				
		45	150				
	8.6.6	46	150				
	8.6.5; 8.6.6	48	151				
	8.6.7	74	161				
	8.6.5	1	111				
		3	111				
	8.6.4	4	111				
	8.6.5	5	111				
	8.6.4	3	113				
	8.6.5	4	113				
	8.6.7	1	115				
		4	115				
	8.6.6	1	117				
	8.6.7	3	117				
	8.6.6	5	117				
		1	118				
	8.6.5	4	119				
	8.6.6	5	119				
	8.6.7	2	111				
	8.6.4	51	152				
		59	154				

Copyright © by Holt, Rinehart and Winston. All rights reserved.

TEST TIPS FOR STUDENTS: READING

The primary goal of the practice in this Reading Test section is to help you prepare for the Grade 9 Indiana Statewide Testing for Educational Progress – plus (*ISTEP+*) and Graduation Qualifying Exam (*ISTEP+ GQE*). This practice will help determine your understanding of different aspects of a reading passage. Basically, if you can grasp the main idea and the author's purpose, and then pay attention to the details and vocabulary so that you are able to draw inferences and conclusions, you will do well on the test.

Strategies for Answering Multiple-Choice Questions

Here are some suggestions for taking any standardized reading test:

- First, **read the passage as if you were not even taking a test.** Do this to get a general overview of both the topic and the tone of a passage.

- **Look at the big picture.** In other words, examine the most obvious features of the passage. To do this, ask yourself the following questions as you read:

    What is the title?

    What do you believe is the main idea of a piece of nonfiction or the theme of a piece of fiction?

    What do you think is the author's purpose? to inform? to entertain? to show how to do something?

- Next, **read the questions.** This will help you to know what information to look for when you re-read.

- Re-read the passage. **Underline information** that relates to the questions. This will help you when filling in the answers.

- **Go back to the questions.** Try to answer each one in your mind before looking at the answer choices.

- Finally, **read *all* the answer choices and eliminate those that are obviously incorrect.** After this process, mark the best answer.

Types of Multiple-Choice Questions

Many multiple-choice questions fall into categories. The following are the most common categories.

1. Main idea: The most important point expressed in a reading passage is the main idea. The main idea must relate to the entire passage, not just to a portion of it. After reading a passage, locate and underline the main idea.

2. Significant details: You will most probably be asked to recall specific details from a reading passage. You will know what details to look for if you read the questions before re-reading the passage. Underline these details as you re-read. Remember that correct answers do not always use the precise phrases or words that appear in the passage.

3. Vocabulary: Standardized tests will often ask you to define a word within the context of the passage. In many instances, the answer choice will include an actual meaning of the word that does not fit the context in which the word appears. Reading the answer choices and then plugging them into the sentence help to determine which answer fits the context of the passage.

4. Conclusion and inference: Standardized tests often want you to draw conclusions or make inferences. There is often some idea within a passage that the author is trying to convey but does not state directly. Sometimes, you must consider various parts of the passage together in order to determine what the author is implying. An answer choice that refers to only one or two sentences or details within the passage is probably not the correct answer.

Other Tips

If you do not understand a passage at first, keep reading. Many times you will find that you know more answers than you first thought. Once you understand the main idea of a passage, you can go from there to figure out the specific information.

As mentioned before, be sure to read *all* of the answer choices before choosing one. Students often make the mistake of rushing through the multiple-choice questions and marking the first answer choice that seems correct. Also, keep in mind that the people who write standardized tests often create incorrect answer choices that are designed to distract you from the right answer. Such "distractors" include answer choices that are true but not relevant to the question, answer choices that relate to the wrong part of the passage, and answer choices that are too broad or too narrow. Finally, read the questions and the answers as carefully as you would read the passage, and you should succeed on the reading sections of standardized tests.

Strategies for Answering Open-Ended Questions

Standardized tests often include open-ended questions, such as short-answer questions and extended-response questions. These questions differ from multiple-choice in that they often ask you to look much more broadly at the reading passage. Open-ended questions test your ability to synthesize what you have learned from reading a passage. Here are some suggestions for answering open-ended questions:

- Read the passage in its entirety. Pay close attention to the major events and characters. Jot down information you believe is central to the passage.

- Read each question carefully. If you cannot answer the question at first, simply skip it and return to it later.

- There are some words that appear frequently in open-ended questions, such as *compare, contrast, interpret, discuss, and summarize.* Be sure you have a complete understanding of these words within the context of the question.

- Return to the passage and skim it. Do this to find the details or examples you need to support your answer.

- When writing the rest of your answer, be precise but brief. Refer to details from the passage. Be sure to proofread for spelling, grammar, and punctuation errors.

TIPS FOR STUDENTS: WRITING

The primary goal of the practice in the Writing section is to help you prepare for the Grade 9 Indiana Statewide Testing for Educational Progress – plus (*ISTEP+*) and Graduation Qualifying Exam (*ISTEP+* GQE). In order to write a concise composition, you must learn to organize your thoughts before you begin writing the actual composition. This keeps you from straying too far from the composition's topic.

Strategies for Answering Composition Questions

- First, **read the question carefully.** Be sure that you understand exactly what the question is asking.

- **Decide what kind of composition you are being asked to write.** You will be asked to write a narrative, informational, descriptive or persuasive composition. **You should ask yourself, "What is the purpose of this composition?"** For example, are you trying to persuade your audience to take an action or to support a position? When you understand the type of composition you are being asked to write, you will have a sense of the purpose of your composition.

- Next, **organize your thoughts.** It is best to write down notes on a separate piece of paper before actually writing the composition. First, determine the main point of your composition. Your topic sentence should include the general topic as well as the main idea. It should set the tone and catch the reader's attention. Most importantly, make sure it is answering the question. This will be the anchor to your composition. Then, come up with ideas to support your topic sentence. Your ideas should include the major points that you want to cover in your composition.

- Write in complete sentences, and be aware of unity within the composition. In other words, make sure your sentences and paragraphs "flow" smoothly. Sentences should come together smoothly to support the main idea and should be arranged in an order that makes sense to the reader. Be as specific as possible when stating your ideas. Make use of transitional words or phrases if necessary. Also, remember to write neatly.

- Finally, **proofread your composition.** Check for spelling and punctuation errors. Look for run-on sentences and sentence fragments. Look over verb tenses to see if you have used them correctly. Make the necessary edits as neat as possible.

If you follow the above guidelines, you should succeed on the writing section of standardized tests. Remember that practice makes perfect. Read and write as often as possible on whatever subjects you prefer, and you will see that writing compositions will eventually come quite naturally.

When It's Test Time...

Here are some final tips for test day.

- Be sure that you are well rested.
- Be on time, and be sure that you have the necessary materials.
- Listen to the instructions of the teacher.
- Read directions and questions carefully.
- Remain calm and remember what you have learned in class, and you should do well.

Good luck!

Reading Test Practice

Reading Test Practice And The Indiana Statewide Testing For Educational Progress-plus (ISTEP+) Test

The Grade 9 *ISTEP+* English/Language Arts Test

In grade nine you will take the Reading Test portion of the *ISTEP+*. This test assesses your readiness for the reading tasks that you will face in the tenth grade.

The *ISTEP+* in Reading

In the reading portion of the *ISTEP+* English/Language Arts Test, you will be given several passages to read. Reading selections will be fiction and nonfiction. The thirty-four questions that follow the reading selections will assess your ability to understand, interpret, and analyze what you have read. Of these thirty-four questions, twenty-seven will be multiple-choice questions, six questions will ask you for a short-answer response, and one question will ask for an extended-response.

Short-answer response items will be scored on the following two-point scale:

Score of 2 Response includes versions of two exemplars.

Score of 1 Response includes version of one exemplar.

Score of 0 Other response.

Extended-response items will be scored on the following four-point scale:

Score of 4 Response fully accomplishes the task, includes many relevant ideas, organizes ideas logically, exhibits very good word usage, demonstrates very good writing technique, with an effective adjustment of language and tone to task and reader.

Score of 3 Response accomplishes the task, includes relevant ideas, organizes ideas logically, exhibits good word usage, demonstrates good writing technique with an attempt to adjust language and tone to task and reader.

Score of 2 Response minimally accomplishes the task, includes some relevant ideas, attempts to organize ideas logically, exhibits ordinary word usage, demonstrates adequate writing technique with an attempt to adjust language and tone to task and reader.

Score of 1 Response partially accomplishes, or fails to accomplish, the task, includes few relevant ideas, exhibits a minimal attempt to organize ideas logically, exhibits minimal word usage, demonstrates minimal or less than minimal writing technique with language and tone that may be inappropriate to task and reader.

Reading Test Practice

On the following pages you will find the reading test practice section: several selections with test questions that are like those on your Indiana test. These questions address the skills and standards that you are expected to master. Preceding these selections and questions are reading strategies and tips that you can use to help you be successful.

STRATEGIES FOR COMPREHENSION

Understanding Main Ideas and Supporting Details

When taking a reading test, you will often be asked to identify a reading selection's main idea. In order to tackle this type of question, follow these steps:

Step 1: Read the selection and determine the topic.

Step 2: Look at what all the details have in common. The details should point to the main idea. **Hint:** Pay attention to the first and last sentences. Sometimes you may find a sentence that states the main idea.

Step 3: State the main idea in your own words. Then, look for an answer that closely matches your own. Be careful not to select a detail that merely *supports* the main idea as your answer.

Step 4: Check to make sure that the details in the selection support your answer.

Identifying Author's Purpose

Reading comprehension tests frequently ask you to identify the author's purpose. While the responses may be specific to the text, each response will usually tie to one of the four general purposes for writing. Use the steps below for help in answering questions about purpose:

Step 1: Look in the text for clues such as the ones below and decide toward which purpose most clues point.

- illustrations, diagrams, maps, charts, headings, and bulleted or numbered items (**to inform**)
- words like *should* and *must,* and words that assign value such as *worst* and *best* (**to influence**)
- frequent use of the word *I* and emotional words (**to express**)
- use of vivid descriptions, dialogue, rhymes, drama, or humor (**to entertain**)

Step 2: Look for the response that most closely matches the general purpose you have identified.

Using Context Clues

As you read a selection in a reading test, you may discover that the author uses unfamiliar words. One way to determine the meaning of an unfamiliar word is to use context clues. A word's context is made up of the words and sentences around it. Use the following steps to answer questions about context clues in a selection:

Step 1: Look at the context of the unfamiliar word. See if the words and sentences around it provide clues to the word's meaning.

Step 2: Use the context clues to make a guess at the unfamiliar word's meaning.

Step 3: Check your definition by inserting it in the passage in place of the unfamiliar word.

Identifying Point of View or Bias

When you read a selection on a reading test, you may be asked to identify the author's point of view or identify any bias. Follow these steps to answer such questions:

Step 1: Determine whether the writer uses more positive words or more negative words.

Step 2: Try to answer the question in your own words.

Step 3: Look for the choice that best matches your own answer.

Summarizing a Text

Standardized reading tests often ask you to identify the best summary of a reading passage. Follow these steps to choose the best answer to a summary question.

Step 1: Look for the main idea and the most important supporting details as you read the passage slowly and carefully.

Step 2: Consider every answer choice, eliminating those that restate a single detail from the passage, make a general statement about the passage but include no important details, or have little or nothing to do with the passage.

Step 3: Be sure that the answer you choose covers the *entire* passage by including the main idea and major supporting details.

Making Inferences

Reading tests often include questions that check your ability to make inferences from a reading passage. Use the following steps to answer inference questions:

Step 1: Skim the passage once for a general understanding; then, re-read it carefully. Keep in mind that most test questions are designed to measure your reading comprehension, not your reading speed.

Step 2: Locate key words and phrases in the answer choices that match similar words and phrases in the reading passage. You may be able to eliminate some answers right away.

Step 3: Confirm your answer by considering your prior knowledge about the subject of the passage.

Predicting Outcomes

Sometimes a reading test will ask you the outcome of events in a narrative passage. Use the following process to determine the *most likely* outcome.

Step 1: Read the passage carefully. Everything you need to know is there. The correct answer must follow easily from the information in the passage—it should never depend on a change in a person or an unlikely turn of events.

Step 2: Using the information in the passage, make a prediction about what will most likely happen next. Ask yourself what will result from the events in the passage.

Step 3: For this kind of question, you will need to read all of the answers before you choose one. Eliminate answers by matching them against what you know from the passage and what you have predicted.

Drawing Conclusions

On a reading test, you may be asked questions that begin like this, "Why do you think..." or "Based on the information in the passage,..." Questions like these require you to draw a conclusion. Use the steps below to respond to these types of questions.

Step 1: Read the question or stem to identify the topic of-the question.

Step 2: Study the answer choices, ruling out those choices that are clearly wrong.

Step 3: Re-read the passage and look for evidence that-supports which of the remaining answer choices is correct.

STRATEGIES FOR ANALYZING AN AUTHOR'S STYLE AND TECHNIQUE

Analyzing Elements of Character, Theme, or Setting

Tests on literature often ask about literary elements such as character, theme, or setting.

Step 1: Be sure you understand the three basic literary elements listed above.

Step 2: As with any reading test, read the questions *before* you read the passage so you know exactly what to look for in the passage.

Step 3: Look for information in the passage that relates to the literary element you are asked to find.

Step 4: Choose the answer that most correctly relates to the details in the passage.

Analyzing Tone

An author's tone is his or her attitude, conveyed largely through word choice. Use the following steps to respond to reading-test questions about author's tone.

Step 1: Look at the writer's diction (word choice). In particular, identify any connotative words the writer uses. Determine what the connotations suggest about the writer's attitude toward the subject.

Step 2: Read all the answer choices, and eliminate those that are clearly inconsistent with what the diction suggests about the writer's tone.

Step 3: Examine the remaining answer choices, and choose the one that best describes the tone of the passage. (Beware of answer choices that exaggerate the writer's attitude.)

Analyzing Style

Some reading test questions will ask you to analyze the author's style. Style refers to the author's unique manner of expression. In addition to tone (see above), mood is a critical element of style. Mood is the feeling that the literature creates. As in tone, the author's diction (word choice) is a major component of mood. Another way to analyze style is to classify it as formal or informal. To answer questions about style, follow the steps below:

Step 1: Look at the answer choices.

- Words like *admiring, bitter,* and *comic* suggest that the question is focusing on tone or mood.
- Words like *slangy, lofty,* or *elevated* suggest that the question is more focused on formality or informality.

Step 2: Eliminate answer choices that are clearly inconsistent with the diction, tone, or mood of the selection.

Step 3: Select the remaining choice that seems most consistent with the diction, tone, or mood of the selection.

Evaluating Rhetorical Strategies

Some tests will test your ability to evaluate rhetorical strategies, including strategies that are not based on solid evidence. One flawed strategy is the use of overgeneralization. Use the following steps to evaluate generalizations you find in your reading.

Step 1: Look for general statements. Words like *no one, never, every,* and *always* may signal a general statement. An example of a general statement that sounds like an overgeneralization is "All dogs love to play in the water."

Step 2: Identify the details that support the statement. If there is no support the statement is probably an overgeneralization.

Step 3: Evaluate the support. Does it really support the broad generalization or only a qualified version of the generalization? An example of an overgeneralization that has been qualified is "Some dogs love to play in the water."

Analyzing Literary Devices

Many tests on literature will ask you to identify literary devices. The chart below reviews some of the major literary devices.

Device and Definition	Example
An **allusion** is a reference to a person, place, or event from history, literature, religion, myth-ology, politics, sport, science, or pop culture.	The George M. Cohan song "The Yankee Doodle Boy" alludes to the eighteenth-century tune "Yankee Doodle."
Figurative language describes one thing in terms of another and is not meant to be taken literally. A **metaphor** compares one thing to something quite unlike it. A **simile** compares two things using like or as. **Personification** describes an inanimate object giving it human characteristics.	**metaphor:** The wind is a rake. **simile:** The thick woods were like prison walls. **personification:** The flower turned its gaze toward the sun.
Imagery is language that appeals to any of the five senses: sight, touch, smell, hearing, and taste.	At the pond, a rustling of dry reeds revealed the brown head of a grackle, who watched the cool, gleaming water with a beady eye.
Irony is the contrast between expectation and reality: between what is said and what is meant (verbal); between what is expected to happen and what really happens (situational); between what a character thinks is true and what the audience knows to be true (dramatic).	**verbal irony:** "Oh, I absolutely *love* that hat. Are those real grapes?" **situational irony:** A solider survives many grueling battles abroad only to be run over by an ice cream truck back home. **dramatic irony:** A play's hero thinks her son is dead, but the audience knows that her son is alive.
A **symbol** is an object, event, person, or animal to which extraordinary meaning is attached.	A skull and crossbones symbolizes danger; red roses symbolize love. These are symbols that everyone uses. Writers try to create fresh symbols.

Read the selection below. Then read each question and choose the best answer. Use the provided answer sheet at the end of the workbook to record your answers, and use a separate sheet of paper to record your response to the open-ended question.

The Railroad Excursion

In 1881, one of the most adventurous ways to travel was by railroad. In that year Ben Travis, age fifteen, took his first long train ride. Ben had ridden aboard trains many times but just for short distances. On this trip Ben traveled with his father from Omaha, Nebraska, to Sacramento, California. They rode the Pacific Express, covering a distance of almost 2,000 miles!

The Express had been in service for a dozen years. Its operation was made possible on that famous date, May 15, 1869, when the rail line was linked up at Promontory, Utah. When the railroad was opened, travel from the Midwest to California was transformed. Instead of taking six months by wagon train, it became possible to get there in less than a week. The train route also affected the number of people making the trip. In the first full year that the line operated, almost 150,000 people rode the train to California. In 1881, nearly a million people made the same trip!

Ben's school semester had just ended, and his father was taking him to spend part of his summer with his grandparents, who lived in San Francisco. When the day came to start their trip, Ben eagerly boarded the train. He made sure he was one of the first passengers to board so he would have a window seat. He didn't want to miss any of the interesting sights along the way.

As they crossed the Great Plains, Ben watched intently for herds of buffalo. Although he sometimes saw a few small herds off in the distance, he never saw the enormous numbers that he had read about in stories. Since the train did not have any dining facilities, it stopped at stations along the way for meals. After several of these stops, Ben and his father were grateful that the trip would last only a few days. The meals, whether breakfast, lunch, or supper, always seemed the same: usually beefsteak, fried potatoes, and fried eggs. Occasionally, there might be an alternative dish, such as the breakfast that some passengers thought was chicken stew but was actually prairie dog.

After crossing the plains, the train began climbing into the higher elevations of the Rocky Mountains. Ben had never seen anything like these mountains. He could look at their endless variety of features and imagine them to be shaped like profiles, stairs, or even castles. There were also any number of small streams, formed from melting snow, flowing down the mountainsides and cascading into waterfalls as they flowed into the larger streams of the valleys.

Ben enjoyed traveling through the mountains more than any other part of the trip, but soon they were in California, nearing the end of the line. After a few more hours they finally arrived at their last stop, Sacramento. Ben found his grandparents waiting on the station platform.

The Railroad Excursion

1. The author's **main** purpose for writing this passage was to

    A describe a train trip long ago.

    B tell about an important event in history.

    C convince people to learn more about railroads.

    D explain why people traveled west in the 1800s.

2. What would **most likely** be different about the way a nonfiction essay would present this topic?

    A It would tell more about the way people felt about the food.

    B It would give more statistics and facts about train travel.

    C It would use more dialogue.

    D It would use more personal anecdotes.

3. How does the second paragraph contribute to the story?

    A It gives the price of tickets.

    B It provides railroad history.

    C It discusses the scenery along the way.

    D It introduces Ben's family.

4. The train stopped at stations along the way to

    A give passengers better views of the scenery.

    B get to California faster.

    C avoid the buffalo.

    D let the passengers eat.

5. Which statement **best** supports the idea that the population of California probably grew in the late 1800s?

    A Ben had never seen anything like these mountains.

    B It was nearly 2,000 miles from Omaha to Sacramento.

    C In 1881, nearly a million people made the same trip.

    D When the railroad was opened, travel from the Midwest to California was transformed.

The Railroad Excursion

6. Which experience is most similar to Ben's experience in the selection?

   A Amy says she likes swim practice even though she really dislikes everything about it.

   B Amy says she dislikes swim practice even though she really likes part of it.

   C Amy says she likes swim practice even though she dislikes two-thirds of the drills.

   D Amy dislikes all the practice drills and says she dislikes swim practice.

7. Based on his actions in the story, which statement is **most likely** true of Ben?

   A Food is not important to him.

   B He is quite prone to motion sickness.

   C He appreciates nature.

   D He thinks prairie dog is delicious.

8. Based on the context of the passage, the word *service* means

   A use.

   B army.

   C dishes.

   D ceremony.

9. Based on the context of the passage, the word *transformed* means

   A difficult.

   B powered.

   C delayed.

   D changed.

10. What does ending the selection with Ben's grandparents waiting on the station platform say about early train travel? Use details from the selection to support your response.

Read the selection below. Then read each question and choose the best answer. Use the provided answer sheet at the end of the workbook to record your answers, and use a separate sheet of paper to record your response to open-ended questions.

A Country Cottage
by Anton Chekhov

Two young people who had not long been married were walking up and down the platform of a little country station. His arm was round her waist, her head was almost on his shoulder, and both were happy.

The moon peeped up from the drifting cloudlets and frowned, as it seemed, envying their happiness. The still air was heavy with the fragrance of lilac and wild cherry. Somewhere in the distance beyond the line a corncrake was calling.

"How beautiful it is, Sasha, how beautiful!" murmured the young wife. "It all seems like a dream. See, how sweet and inviting that little copse looks! How nice those solid, silent telegraph posts are! They add a special note to the landscape, suggesting humanity, civilization in the distance. . . . Don't you think it's lovely when the wind brings the rushing sound of a train?"

"Yes. . . . But . . . What have you got for our supper to-night?"

"Chicken and salad. . . . It's a chicken just big enough for two. . . . Then there is the salmon and sardines that were sent from town."

(6) The moon hid her face behind a cloud. Human happiness reminded her of her own loneliness, of her solitary couch beyond the hills and dales.

"The train is coming!" said Varya, "how jolly!"

Three eyes of fire could be seen in the distance. The stationmaster came out on the platform. Signal lights flashed here and there on the line.

"Let's see the train in and go home," said Sasha, yawning. "What a splendid time we are having together, Varya, it's so splendid, one can hardly believe it's true!"

The dark monster crept noiselessly alongside the platform and came to a standstill. They caught glimpses of sleepy faces, of hats and shoulders at the dimly lighted windows.

"Look! look!" they heard from one of the carriages. "Varya and Sasha have come to meet us! There they are! . . . Varya! . . . Varya. . . . Look!"

Two little girls skipped out of the train and hung on Varya's neck. They were followed by a stout, middle-aged lady, and a tall, lanky gentleman with grey whiskers; behind them came two schoolboys, laden with bags, and after the schoolboys, the governess, after the governess the grandmother.

"Here we are, here we are, dear boy!" began the whiskered gentleman, squeezing Sasha's hand. "Sick of waiting for us, I expect! You have been pitching into your old uncle for not coming down all this time, I daresay! Kolya, Kostya, Nina, Fifa . . . children! Kiss your cousin Sasha! We're all here, the whole troop of us, just for three or four days. . . . I hope we shan't be too many for you? You mustn't let us put you out!"

(14) At the sight of their uncle and his family, the young couple were horror-stricken. While his uncle talked and kissed them, Sasha had a vision of their little cottage: he and Varya giving up their three little rooms, all the pillows and bedding to

their guests; the salmon, the sardines, the chicken all devoured in a single instant; the cousins plucking the flowers in their little garden, spilling the ink, filling the cottage with noise and confusion; his aunt talking continually about her ailments and her papa's having been Baron von Fintich. . . .

And Sasha looked almost with hatred at his young wife, and whispered: "It's you they've come to see!"

"No, it's you," answered Varya, pale with anger. "They're your relations! they're not mine!"

And turning to her visitors, she said with a smile of welcome: "Welcome to the cottage!"

(18) The moon came out again. She seemed to smile, as though she were glad she had no relations. Sasha, turning his head away to hide his angry despairing face, struggled to give a note of cordial welcome to his voice as he said:

"It is jolly of you! Welcome to the cottage!"

A Country Cottage

1. Which terms **best** describe how Sasha and Varya feel at the beginning of the story?

   A   realistic and practical

   B   insecure and lonely

   C   quiet and peaceful

   D   blissful and romantic

2. In this passage from the second paragraph, "The moon peeped up from the drifting cloudlets and frowned, . . ." the author uses

   A   allusion.

   B   simile.

   C   personification.

   D   alliteration.

3. Which of the following foreshadows the approaching conflict?

   A   "The still air was heavy with the fragrance of lilac and wild cherry."

   B   "The dark monster crept noiselessly alongside the platform. . . ."

   C   "The stationmaster came out on the platform."

   D   "They caught glimpses of sleepy faces, of hats and shoulders at the dimly lighted windows."

4. Based on his comments in the selection, which statement is **most likely** true of Sasha?

   A   He will treat his wife badly.

   B   He sees cooking as "the wife's" duty.

   C   He views the world as poetically as does Varya.

   D   He hates his relatives.

A Country Cottage

5. Which characteristic **best** describes the visiting relatives' understanding of Sasha and Varya's feelings about having guests?

    A oblivious

    B angry

    C embarrassed

    D appalled

6. When the relatives arrive, what do Sasha and Varya's words and actions reveal?

    A They both feel that honesty is the best policy.

    B They both set firm limits for their relatives about the timing and length of visits.

    C They recognize the importance of family ties and genuinely welcome their visitors.

    D They would rather take out their resentment on each other than show disrespect to their relatives.

7. In the context of the third paragraph, the word *copse* **most likely** means

    A a comfortable stuffed chair.

    B a group of small trees.

    C a gathering of teenagers.

    D a dish of shrimp and rice.

8. With which theme of the story would the moon would agree?

    A The sweetness of a couple in love can turn bitter when relatives arrive.

    B It is more important to honor one's relatives than to strive for romantic love.

    C It never pays to hang around out of doors after dark.

    D Flexibility is the main key to success in marriage.

A Country Cottage

9. In the chart below, write meanings of the words in the context of the given paragraphs.

Word	Paragraph	Meaning
solitary	6	
ailments	14	
cordial	18	

10. What is the *main* conflict for Varya and Sasha in the story? Use details from the selection to support your response.

Read the selection below. Then read each question and choose the best answer. Use the provided answer sheet at the end of the workbook to record your answers, and use a separate sheet of paper to record your response to open-ended questions.

from *My Ántonia*, Book I, Part VI
Willa Cather

Much as I liked Ántonia, I hated a superior tone that she sometimes took with me. She was four years older than I, to be sure, and had seen more of the world; but I was a boy and she was a girl, and I resented her protecting manner. Before the autumn was over, she began to treat me more like an equal and to defer to me in other things than reading lessons. This change came about from an adventure we had together.

One day when I rode over to the Shimerdas' I found Ántonia starting off on foot for Russian Peter's house, to borrow a spade Ambrosch needed....

We found Russian Peter digging his potatoes. We were glad to go in and get warm by his kitchen stove and to see his squashes and Christmas melons, heaped in the storeroom for winter. As we rode away with the spade, Ántonia suggested that we stop at the prairie-dog town[1] and dig into one of the holes. We could find out whether they ran straight down, or were horizontal, like mole holes; whether they had underground connections; whether the owls had nests down there, lined with feathers. We might get some puppies, or owl eggs, or snake skins.

The dog town was spread out over perhaps ten acres. The grass had been nibbled short and even, so this stretch was not shaggy and red like the surrounding country, but gray and velvety. The holes were several yards apart, and were disposed[2] with a good deal of regularity, almost as if the town had been laid out in streets and avenues. One always felt that an orderly and very sociable kind of life was going on there.....We went wandering about, looking for a hole that would be easy to dig. The dogs were out, as usual, dozens of them, sitting up on their hind legs over the doors of their houses. As we approached, they barked, shook their tails at us, and scurried underground....

We were examining a big hole with two entrances. The burrow sloped into the ground at a gentle angle, so that we could see where the two corridors united, and the floor was dusty from use, like a little highway over which much travel went. I was walking backward, in a crouching position, when I heard Ántonia scream. She was standing opposite me, pointing behind me and shouting something in Bohemian. I whirled round, and there ... was the biggest snake I had ever seen. He was sunning himself, after the cold night, and he must have been asleep when Ántonia screamed. When I turned, he was lying in long loose waves, like a letter "W." He twitched and began to coil slowly. He was not merely a big snake, I thought—he was a circus monstrosity. His abominable[3] muscularity, his loathsome, fluid motion, somehow made me sick. He was as thick as my leg, and looked as if millstones couldn't crush the disgusting vitality out of him. He lifted his hideous little head,

---

1. **prairie-dog town:** Prairie dogs are not dogs but burrowing rodents who make their underground homes, called towns, all over the Great Plains of North America.
2. **disposed:** positioned.
3. **abominable:** causing disgust or hatred.

and rattled. I didn't run because I didn't think of it—if my back had been against a stone wall I couldn't have felt more cornered. I saw his coils tighten—now he would spring, spring his length, I remembered. I ran up and drove at his head with my spade, struck him fairly across the neck, and in a minute he was all about my feet in wavy loops. I struck now from hate. Ántonia, barefooted as she was, ran up behind me. Even after I had pounded his ugly head flat, his body kept on coiling and winding, doubling and falling back on itself. I walked away and turned my back. I felt seasick.

Ántonia came after me, crying, "O Jimmy, he not bite you? You sure? Why you not run when I say?"

"What did you jabber Bohunk[4] for? You might have told me there was a snake behind me!" I said petulantly.

"I know I am just awful, Jim, I was so scared." She took my handkerchief from my pocket and tried to wipe my face with it, but I snatched it away from her. I suppose I looked as sick as I felt.

"I never know you was so brave, Jim," she went on comfortingly. "You is just like big mans; you wait for him lift his head and then you go for him. Ain't you feel scared a bit? Now we take that snake home and show everybody. Nobody ain't seen in this kawntree so big snake like you kill."

She went on in this strain[5] until I began to think that I had longed for this opportunity, and had hailed it with joy. Cautiously we went back to the snake; he was still groping with his tail, turning up his ugly belly in the light. A faint, fetid[6] smell came from him, and a thread of green liquid oozed from his crushed head.

"Look, Tony, that's his poison," I said. . . .

The sun had set when we reached our garden and went down the draw[7] toward the house. Otto Fuchs was the first one we met. He was sitting on the edge of the cattle-pond, having a quiet pipe before supper. Ántonia called him to come quick and look. He did not say anything for a minute, but scratched his head and turned the snake over with his boot.

"Where did you run onto that beauty, Jim?"

"Up at the dog-town," I answered laconically[8].

"Kill him yourself? How come you to have a weapon?"

"We'd been up to Russian Peter's, to borrow a spade for Ambrosch."

Otto shook the ashes out of his pipe and squatted down to count the rattles. "It was just luck you had a tool," he said cautiously. "Gosh! I wouldn't want to do any business with that fellow myself, unless I had a fence-post along. Your grandmother's snake-cane wouldn't more than tickle him. He could stand right up and talk to you, he could. Did he fight hard?"

Ántonia broke in: "He fight something awful! He is all over Jimmy's boots. I scream for him to run, but he just hit and hit that snake like he was crazy."

Otto winked at me. After Ántonia rode on he said: "Got him in the head first crack, didn't you? That was just as well."

We hung him up to the windmill, and when I went down to the kitchen, I found Ántonia standing in the middle of the floor, telling the story with a great deal of color.

Subsequent experiences with rattle-snakes taught me that my first encounter

---

4. **bohunk:** slang for Bohemian, a dialect of the Czech language.
5. **she went on in this strain:** she kept talking this way.
6. **fetid:** bad-smelling.
7. **draw:** shallow area.
8. **laconically:** using few words.

was fortunate in circumstance. My big rattler was old, and had led too easy a life; there was not much fight in him. He had probably lived there for years, with a fat prairie-dog for breakfast whenever he felt like it, a sheltered home, even an owl-feather bed, perhaps, and he had forgot that the world doesn't owe rattlers a living. A snake of his size, in fighting trim, would be more than any boy could handle. So in reality it was a mock adventure; the game was fixed for me by chance, as it probably was for many a dragon-slayer. I had been adequately armed by Russian Peter; the snake was old and lazy; and I had Ántonia beside me, to appreciate and admire.

That snake hung on our corral fence for several days; some of the neighbors came to see it and agreed that it was the biggest rattler ever killed in those parts. This was enough for Ántonia. She liked me better from that time on, and she never took a supercilious[9] air with me again. I had killed a big snake—I was now a big fellow.

---
9. **supercilious:** acting superior, haughty.

from **My Ántonia, Book I, Part VI**

1. What is the ***most likely*** reason that Ántonia wipes Jim's face with a handkerchief?

   A The snake has bitten his face.

   B He has thrown up on himself.

   C He is sweating and possibly tearful.

   D He accidentally struck his nose with the spade.

2. Which of the following ***best*** describes Ántonia's manner as she recounts the story of the snake?

   A She is shaken and prefers not to dwell on it.

   B She tells it calmly and objectively, like a news reporter.

   C She tells it dishonestly in a way that highlights her role.

   D She tells it enthusiastically, adding color and detail.

3. Which of these statements from the fourth paragraph is ***most likely*** an example of exaggeration?

   A The dog town was spread out over perhaps ten acres.

   B The holes were several yards apart, and were disposed with a good deal of regularity, almost as if the town had been laid out in streets and avenues.

   C One always felt that an orderly and very sociable kind of life was going on there.

   D As we approached, they barked, shook their tails at us, and scurried underground.

4. In the context of the first paragraph, what does the word *defer* mean?

   A to postpone until a later date

   B to skin or remove the fur from

   C to bow to another's opinion

   D to direct, as for treatment or information

from **My Ántonia, Book I, Part VI**

5. Based on his thoughts in the second to last paragraph, which statement is *most likely* true of Jim?

   A   He was conceited.

   B   He was sappy.

   C   He was a dreamer.

   D   He was level-headed.

6. Which of the following describes one method the author uses in this excerpt to hint at characters' backgrounds and help illustrate the story's setting?

   A   She includes details about clothes.

   B   She reproduces the characters' dialects.

   C   She has the characters talk about their backgrounds.

   D   She includes all characters' inner thoughts.

7. What is the effect of the use of first person in this selection?

   A   It shows that Jim knew more about the situation than Ántonia knew.

   B   It allows the author to use more descriptive language.

   C   It shows that the author did some research before writing.

   D   It helps the reader understand the author's feelings and thoughts.

8. In the story, Otto describes the snake in this way.

   "Gosh! I wouldn't want to do any business with that fellow myself, unless I had a fence-post along. Your gandmother's snake-cane wouldn't more than tickle him. He could stand right up and talk to you, he could. Did he fight hard?"

   What literary technique does the writer use here?

   A   personification

   B   foreshadowing

   C   simile

   D   metaphor

from *My Ántonia,* Book I, Part VI

9. What does the snake symbolize in this story? Explain your answer with evidence from the story.

10. What is *most* ironic about how Jim viewed the event with the snake compared to how others' viewed it? Use details from the story to support your response.

Read the selection below. Then read each question and choose the best answer. Use the provided answer sheet at the end of the workbook to record your answers, and use a separate sheet of paper to record your response to open-ended questions.

from Three Soldiers
by John Dos Passos

In his novel Three Solders, Dos Passos describes the experiences of three fictional U.S. soldiers fighting in Europe during World War I. This excerpt introduces two of these soldiers, Chrisfield and John Andrews.

Chrisfield—
"Where's the artillery? That's what I want to know," cried the lieutenant, suddenly stopping in his tracks and running a hand through his red hair. "Where's the artillery?" He looked at Chrisfield savagely out of green eyes. "No use advancing without artillery." He started walking faster than ever.

All at once they saw sunlight ahead of them and olive-drab uniforms. Machine guns started firing all around them in a sudden gust. Chrisfield found himself running forward across a field full of stubble and sprouting clover among a group of men he did not know. The whip-like sound of rifles had chimed in with the stuttering of the machine guns. Little white clouds sailed above him in a blue sky, and in front of him was a group of houses that had the same color, white with lavender-grey shadows, as the clouds.

He was in a house, with a grenade like a tin pineapple in each hand. The sudden loneliness frightened him again. Outside the house was a sound of machine-gun firing, broken by the occasional bursting of a shell. . . . He was in a small kitchen. . . . At the other end of the kitchen, beyond two broken chairs, was a door. . . . Holding in his breath, he stood a long time looking at the door. Then he pulled it open recklessly. A young man with fair hair was sitting at a table, his head resting on his hands. Chrisfield felt a spurt of joy when he saw that the man's uniform was green [German]. Very coolly he pressed the spring, held the grenade a second and then threw it, throwing himself backwards into the middle of the kitchen.

Andrews—
There were tiny green frogs in one of the putty-colored puddles by the roadside. John Andrews fell out of the slowly advancing column a moment to look at them. The frogs' triangular heads stuck out of the water in the middle of the puddle. He leaned over, his hands on his knees, easing the weight of the equipment on his back. That way he could see their tiny jewelled eyes, topaz-colored. . . . Something was telling him that he must run forward and fall into line again, that he must shamble[1] on through the mud, but he remained staring at the puddle, watching the frogs. Then he noticed his reflection in the puddle. He looked at it curiously. He could barely see the outlines of a stained grimacing mask, and the silhouette of the gun barrel slanting behind it. So this was what they had made of him. . . .

Absently, as if he had no connection with all that went on about him, he heard the twang of bursting shrapnel down the road. He had straightened himself wearily and taken a step forward, when he found himself sinking into the puddle. A feeling

---
1. **shamble:** walk unsteadily

of relief came over him. His legs sunk in the puddle; he lay without moving against the muddy bank. The frogs had gone, but from somewhere a little stream of red was creeping out slowly into the putty-colored water. He watched the irregular files of men in olive-drab shambling by. . . . He felt triumphantly separated from them, as if he were in a window somewhere watching soldiers pass, or in a box of a theater watching some dreary monotonous play.

from **Three Soldiers**

1. To which sense do the descriptions in the second paragraph *mostly* appeal?

   A sight

   B smell

   C hearing

   D touch

2. What is the effect of having Chrisfield notice white clouds and Andrews watching frogs?

   A to show that neither of them is paying attention to what they are doing

   B to show their craving for normalcy

   C to show that neither of them are good soldiers

   D to show that Chrisfield is creative and Andrews is sensitive

3. How do small details, such as noting that the lieutenant had red hair and green eyes, contribute to the story?

   A They are filler details that help a story spread out and last longer.

   B They help to clarify the nationality of the soldiers.

   C They make the story less sad and depressing.

   D They make the story and the war feel very personal.

4. The phrase *like a tin pineapple* is an example of a(n)

   A analogy.

   B hyperbole.

   C simile.

   D personification.

from **Three Soldiers**

5. Which statement ***best*** supports the idea that Dos Pasos views war as causing an absence of normal human responses?

   A   He shows the lieutenant as frustrated when he realizes they have no artillery.

   B   He writes that Chrisfield felt joy upon seeing and planning to kill an enemy soldier.

   C   He portrays Andrews as finding frog eyes interesting.

   D   He describes Chrisfield as running when the machine guns start blasting.

6. In the context of the last sentence, the word *monotonous* means

   A   unvarying.

   B   shuffling.

   C   crimson.

   D   vivacious.

7. Read this sentence from the fourth paragraph of the passage. What feelings are conveyed by the sentence?

   So this was what they had made of him . . .

   A   boredom

   B   confusion

   C   surprise

   D   despair

from **Three Soldiers**

8. Complete this chart with the two requested summaries.

Write a brief summary telling what happens to Chrisfield.	
Write a brief summary telling what happens to Andrews.	

9. Why do you think Andrews is relieved at the sensation of sinking into the puddle?

10. Does the author seem to approve of one man over the other? Explain.

Read the selection below. Then read each question and choose the best answer. Use the provided answer sheet at the end of the workbook to record your answers, and use a separate sheet of paper to record your response to open-ended questions.

Space Junk

For the past forty years or so, we have heard much about the accomplishments of the first people to fly in space, orbit the earth, land on the moon, and live and work on a space station. We often receive news about the latest photographs from space telescopes and probes sent to explore distant planets. However, there is one aspect of the human exploration of space about which we hear very little, even though it may eventually become a serious problem for future space missions. This is the phenomenon of space junk. Almost every time a rocket or satellite is launched into space, bits and pieces have fallen off or have been deliberately jettisoned. These rocket pieces now form a vast orbiting array of debris.

Tiny particles of debris, no larger than a marble, are estimated to number in the millions! These particles include fragments as small as the chips of paint that flake off rockets because of extreme heat and cold. However, even these minuscule bits of matter can pose a problem because each particle is traveling at about 18,000 miles per hour! They can scratch and damage a space shuttle's windows, which are generally replaced after each mission for this very reason.

Slightly larger pieces of matter, up to the size of a small grapefruit, are estimated to number about 100,000. Pieces of even larger debris are so potentially dangerous that the U.S. Space Surveillance Network monitors each and every one of them. By 1998, the network was tracking approximately 9,000 such objects and is expecting a huge increase in years to come as more and more satellites are launched. The network trackers assign a number to each large piece of space junk, and they know its location at all times. If a piece falls to Earth, as all of them eventually will, the network can cross it off the list. We don't need to worry much about most of these objects because they burn up from the friction of reentry into Earth's atmosphere. However, very large pieces could survive reentry and crash somewhere on Earth.

To understand the nature of the situation more clearly, remember that Earth is rotating at a high rate of speed. If an object matches or exceeds the speed of Earth's rotation, the object will stay in orbit for at least a while. Objects in low-altitude orbit, 200–300 miles above ground, generally fall within a year or two. Every decade or so an increase in solar activity heats and expands the upper atmosphere, thus causing objects at altitudes up to 400 miles to plummet. However, objects 500 miles or more above the surface will remain in orbit for centuries. It is estimated that satellites that are more than 20,000 miles up will not come down for millions of years.

A major concern is the danger of a fairly large object colliding with a spacecraft or communication satellite. On one occasion, this actually happened. A French satellite was launched in 1986; the rocket that propelled it was discarded and became a large piece of space junk. Nine months later it was observed exploding into thousands of pieces. About five hundred of those pieces were large enough to track. In July 1996, one of those pieces, Satellite No. 18,208, struck another French satellite and chopped off a section of it.

While that was the only known direct hit, there have been several alarming close calls. In August 1997, a 500-pound rocket motor that had been in orbit for more than twelve years came within two miles of a multimillion-dollar research satellite that was following the space shuttle *Discovery*. Even more frightening, in September 1997, an old U.S. military satellite came within a thousand yards of the Russian space station *Mir,* causing the two Russian cosmonauts and one U.S. astronaut aboard to prepare for an emergency evacuation.

One proposed solution to the problem is to develop Earth-based lasers that will obliterate the chunks of debris before they can do any harm. Already, shuttle missions are carefully planned to avoid encounters with space junk. Clearly, this is a problem that will have to be faced in the future.

Space Junk

1. What is the *main* idea of the selection?

    A   The U.S. Space program needs to be shut down.

    B   We must deal with the problem of debris that orbits Earth.

    C   The use of satellites has helped humanity in many ways.

    D   It is dangerous to use lasers in space.

2. What is the *main* purpose of this selection?

    A   to convince readers to become astronauts

    B   to tell an intriguing story about space

    C   to inform readers about a problem

    D   to criticize the U.S. space program

3. Read this summary of the first paragraph.

    We hear a lot about our accomplishments in space, but we hear little about space junk.

    Which statement *best* completes the summary?

    A   No one really cares about space travel, anyway.

    B   Space junk is going to make space travel impossible.

    C   Rocket pieces float in space.

    D   Space junk is likely to become a serious problem.

4. Why are the words "Discovery" and "Mir" in italics in the selection?

    A   to signal readers to skip over them since they do not make sense where they are used

    B   to show that they are subtitles in this selection

    C   to show that they are proper names of a shuttle and a space station

    D   to signal the beginning of a new topic

Space Junk

5. How does the connotation of *junk* help the writer make his or her point?

    A   It makes people think of garbage and may even remind the reader of problems with too much garbage here on Earth.

    B   People like to collect junk.

    C   It helps people compare the spacecraft with broken down cars.

    D   It reminds the reader of garage sales.

6. Based on the context of the first paragraph, the word *jettisoned* means

    A   followed.

    B   discarded.

    C   orbited.

    D   invented.

7. Which of the following **best** summarizes the next-to last paragraph?

    A   Space is full of dangerous debris.

    B   Large orbiting objects are tracked.

    C   A piece of space junk once hit a satellite.

    D   There have been a number of near misses.

8. Which is the **best** evidence that the situation described in the passage is serious?

    A   It affects satellite equipment and human lives.

    B   It has been going on for more than forty years.

    C   The author was concerned enough to write about it.

    D   Plans are being considered to deal with the situation.

9. Why does the author begin the selection in the first person?

10. What problem faces the windows on space shuttles and how is this possible problem addressed?

Read the selection below. Then read each question and choose the best answer. Use the provided answer sheet at the end of the workbook to record your answers, and use a separate sheet of paper to record your response to the open-ended question.

To a Locomotive In Winter
by Walt Whitman

Thee for my recitative[1],
Thee in the driving storm even as now, the snow, the winter-day declining,
Thee in thy panoply[2], thy measur'd dual throbbing and thy beat convulsive,
Thy black cylindric body, golden brass and silvery steel,
Thy ponderous side-bars, parallel and connecting rods, gyrating, shuttling at thy sides,
Thy metrical, now swelling pant and roar, now tapering in the distance,
Thy great protruding headlight fix'd in front,
Thy long, pale, floating vapor-pennants, tinged with delicate purple,
The dense and murky clouds out-belching from thy smoke-stack.
Thy knitted frame, thy springs and valves, the tremulous twinkle of thy wheels,
Thy train of cars behind, obedient, merrily following,
Through gale or calm, now swift, now slack, yet steadily careening[3];
Type of the modern - emblem of motion and power - pulse of the continent,
For once come serve the Muse and and merge in verse, even as here I see thee,
With storm and buffeting gusts of wind and falling snow,
By day thy warning ringing bell to sound its notes,
By night thy silent signal lamps to swing.

Fierce-throated beauty!
Roll through my chant with all thy lawless music,thy swinging lamps at night,
Thy piercing, madly-whistled laughter, thy echoes, rumbling like an earthquake, rousing all,
Law of thyself complete, thine old track firmly holding,
(No sweetness debonair[4] of tearful harp or glib[5] piano thine,)
Thy trills and shrieks by rocks and hills return'd,
Launch'd o'er the prairies wide, across the lakes,
To the free skies unpent and glad and strong.

---

1. **recitative:** piece for public performance
2. **panoply:** splendid display
3. **careening:** rushing
4. **debonair:** carefree
5. **glib:** easy

To a Locomotive In Winter

1. Which of these phrases *best* describes the appearance of the locomotive?

   A   Thy black cylindric body, golden brass and silvery steel,

   B   Thy metrical, now swelling pant and roar, now tapering in the distance,

   C   Thee for my recitative

   D   Through gale or calm, now swift, now slack, yet steadily careening

2. The poet says that the train's "law of [itself is] complete" to

   A   show that there were many legal problems with the locomotive.

   B   show that the locomotive was a self-powered.

   C   show that, after years of work, the locomotive was ready to run.

   D   emphasize its miraculous technology.

3. Why does Whitman call the locomotive the "pulse of the continent"?

   A   The train vibrates the Earth as it moves along.

   B   He sees it as a symbol of the technological progress of the country.

   C   He believes everyone is fascinated by trains.

   D   He thinks it will be the downfall of the young country.

4. Why do you suppose Whitman focuses on the train during winter rather than another season?

   A   to show that the train had a heater that worked well

   B   to show that the train could provide year-round transportation

   C   to show the train's ability to hurdle adversity

   D   to show that spring and summer were lesser seasons

To a Locomotive In Winter

5. In what ways does Whitman present the locomotive as a symbol of the industrial United States of the 1800s?

   A He showed that it was loud and noisy.

   B He showed that the train was a financial success.

   C He explained how the locomotive was built.

   D He depicted it as an emblem of motion and power.

6. In the context of the poem, what does the term *fierce-throated* mean?

   A sickly and sore

   B loud and powerful

   C choking

   D frightening

7. What is *most likely* the *theme* of this poem?

   A the power of technology

   B the strength of love

   C fear of change

   D the endurance of nature

8. How would you *most* expect a poem written today to differ from this poem written in the 1800s?

   A It would not describe prairies and lakes.

   B It would rhyme.

   C It would not praise smoke and loud noise.

   D It would be shorter.

9. How is this poem *most like* an *ode*?

   A It could easily be set to music.

   B It is a long poem that describes the heroic deeds of men who built trains.

   C It tells a story.

   D It praises the great railroads.

10. What point of view is the poem written in and what is its effect?

Read the selection below. Then read each question and choose the best answer. Use the provided answer sheet at the end of the workbook to record your answers, and use a separate sheet of paper to record your response to open-ended questions.

Pangaea

As explorers such as Columbus and Magellan sailed the oceans of the world, they brought back information about new continents and their coastlines. Mapmakers used the information to make the first reliable world maps. As people studied the maps, they were impressed by the similarity of the continental shorelines on either side of the Atlantic Ocean. The continents looked as though they would fit together, like the parts of a giant jigsaw puzzle. Were the continents once part of the same huge landmass? If so, what caused this landmass to break apart? What caused the continents to move to their present locations? These questions eventually led to the formulation of hypotheses.

In 1912, a German scientist, Alfred Wegener, proposed a hypothesis called continental drift, which stated that the continents had moved. Wegener hypothesized that the continents once formed part of a single giant landmass, which he named Pangaea, meaning "all lands." In addition to the similarities in the coastlines of the continents, Wegener soon found other evidence to support his hypothesis. If the continents had once been joined, research should uncover fossils of the same plants and animals in areas that had been adjoining parts of Pangaea. Wegener knew that identical fossil remains had already been found in both eastern South America and western Africa. The age and type of rocks in coastal regions of widely separated areas, such as western Africa and eastern Brazil, matched closely.

Despite the evidence supporting the hypothesis of continental drift, Wegener's ideas met with strong opposition. The conclusive evidence that Wegener sought to support his hypothesis was finally discovered in 1947. As scientists examined rock samples that they brought up from the ocean floor, they made a startling discovery. None of the oceanic rocks were more than 150 million years old. The oldest continental rocks are about 4 billion years old. Here, at last, were the discoveries that Wegener had sought. They provided the scientific evidence he needed to formulate the theory of continental drift.

Pangaea

1. The author uses a series of questions at the end of the first paragraph to

    A show that the information is still unknown.

    B give the feel of real people thinking about an idea.

    C make it easier to write about the ideas.

    D quote the exact questions that were asked.

2. People started to notice that continental coastlines on either side of the Atlantic bore striking similarities

    A during biblical times.

    B since Columbus's time.

    C in 1912.

    D in 1947.

3. Which statement *best* supports the theory of continental drift?

    A Since the oceanic rocks are younger than continental rock, they must have formed after the continents drifted apart.

    B Since the oceanic rocks are older than the continental rock, they must have been submerged until Pangaea broke up.

    C Since the oceanic rocks are older than the continental rock, a meteorite must have deposited them there.

    D Heat released from the formation of oceanic rock must have caused the continents to split apart.

4. Which of the following pieces of evidence does *not* support the theory of continental drift?

    A the similarities of the coastlines on either side of the Atlantic

    B the age of rock on the ocean floor

    C the vastly different plant and animal species on different continents

    D the identical fossil remains found in eastern South America and western Africa

Pangaea

5. Which of the following words shares a common word part with the word *Pangaea*?

   A geology

   B pantheon

   C geopolitics

   D all of the above

6. Based on the information in the article, how is a hypothesis different from a theory?

   A A hypothesis is always met with strong opposition.

   B A hypothesis is supported by fossil records, carbon dating, and rock samples.

   C A theory eventually leads to the formulation of a hypothesis.

   D A theory is supported by conclusive evidence.

7. Based on the passage, it is *most likely* that the continents began to drift apart

   A about 150 million years ago.

   B over 4 billion years ago.

   C in 1912.

   D 100 years ago.

8. Which of these questions could *most likely* be answered by doing further research on this topic?

   A What would prehistoric people have thought about the separation of Pangaea?

   B What were Alfred Wegener's qualifications as a scientist?

   C Will the continents ever reconnect?

   D What will it take for the continents to separate even more?

9. Briefly explain the theory of continental drift.

Pangaea

10. Complete this chart by writing a purpose and a main idea for the selection.

Main Purpose	
Main Idea	

Read the selection below. Then read each question and choose the best answer. Use the provided answer sheet at the end of the workbook to record your answers, and use a separate sheet of paper to record your response to open-ended questions.

From Dream to Disaster

On a calm, starry night in 1912, the largest ship that had ever been built struck an iceberg. In less than three hours the ship plunged to the bottom of the Atlantic Ocean. The first voyage of the R.M.S. *Titanic* had ended, and more than 1,500 people lost their lives.

When the *Titanic* began the voyage from England to New York, many people on board believed the massive ship was unsinkable. Passengers thought they were sailing on the safest ship afloat, a masterpiece of technology. Strong and sleek, the *Titanic* was constructed of forty-six thousand tons of steel. It had a hull with a double bottom, unlike most ships. For extra safety the hull was divided into sixteen watertight compartments, which were separated by locked doors. Water could flood four of the compartments, and the ship would still float. The ship's designers thought the worst collision would only damage two compartments. What series of events could have doomed the mighty *Titanic*?

The *Titanic* set sail on April 10, 1912. Four days later, the ship's radio operators received seven warnings from other ships about icebergs in the area. The *Titanic* had no procedure for relaying messages from the radio operators to the captain. The warning messages were received by several different radio operators. Not all of the messages reached Captain Smith. The night of April 14, the *Titanic* steamed ahead almost at full speed.

Late that evening, the *Titanic* arrived in the radio range of Canada. For the first time, passengers could send messages to their families in the United States. The last, most important iceberg warning came at 10:55 p.m., but the radio operator was busy sending passengers' personal messages. He never reported the iceberg warning to the captain. Lookouts were posted in the crow's-nest high above the ship. Usually they had binoculars, but that night they did not. They strained their eyes searching the cold, moonless dark. The sea was calm and silent. In a rougher sea, they might have spotted waves splashing against the enormous, white iceberg and called out a warning in time.

At around 11:40 p.m., a lookout rang the alarm bell and telephoned the officers on the bridge. "Iceberg right ahead!" he yelled. The first officer ordered the crew to turn the ship away from the iceberg, and then he switched the doors closed in the watertight compartments. If the ship had turned away at full speed, it might have missed the iceberg. Instead, the first officer sent a signal to stop and reverse the engines, which slowed the ship down. The right side of the *Titanic* scraped against the iceberg. The jolt was slight, but the damage was serious. Ice rammed against the seams of the hull where rivets held together the steel plates. The rivets loosened and popped out. The plates separated, and water began pouring into the hull. The engineers turned on the pumps right away, but the sea flooded in too fast for the pumps to keep up. The doors of the watertight compartments were truly watertight, but the walls between the compartments were open at the tops. When one compartment flooded, water spilled over into the next one. The compartments resembled an ice cube tray tilted into a sink of water. It was only a matter of time before all the compartments flooded, and the ship nose-dived into the deep.

The *Titanic* carried more than 2,200 passengers but only enough lifeboats for 1,178 people. Even with the lifeboats, only around 700 people survived the disaster. The crew sent out distress signals by radio and fired white rockets into the night sky. The one ship close enough to help, the *Californian*, sat less than twenty miles away.

Unfortunately, its operator had turned off the radio for the night and had gone to sleep. The sinking of the *Titanic* horrified the world. In 1913, the first International Convention for Safety of Life at Sea created new rules. The rules required ships to carry enough lifeboats for every person on board and to hold lifeboat drills on every voyage. Ships had to keep a radio watch twenty-four hours a day, every day. The legacy of the *Titanic* became one not only of death and loss, but of life and safety for all who sail.

From Dream to Disaster

1. What is the **main** purpose of this selection?

    A to tell a *Titanic* survivor's version of events

    B to persuade readers to think twice before getting on a ship

    C to describe the sinking of the *Titanic* and its consequences

    D to express the author's sense of sorrow

2. How do the first five words help set the mood for the first part of the selection?

    A The words make it clear that the mood will soon be frantic.

    B The words describe both the night and the people's attitudes about the *Titanic*.

    C The words show that the story is just a fairy tale with fairy tale characters.

    D The words show that the weather is nice so the passengers are in a good mood.

3. The effect of beginning the selection with key information about the sinking of the *Titanic* is to

    A provide readers with background.

    B establish the setting.

    C create a picture in the readers' minds.

    D build suspense.

4. The effect of including the direct quotation in paragraph 5 is to

    A emphasize the truthfulness of the author's account.

    B show that the author has conducted serious research.

    C build suspense for the readers.

    D suggest that the lookout had not done his job properly.

5. Which adjective **best** describes the designers of the *Titanic*?

    A pleasant

    B romantic

    C polite

    D confident

From Dream to Disaster

6. According to the selection, which statement about the sinking of *Titanic* is **most likely** true?

    A The sinking was the most important event in the twentieth century.

    B The sinking made many people choose air travel rather than ocean travel.

    C The sinking actually helped make ocean travel safer.

    D The sinking caused ocean travelers to use routes where they would not see icebergs.

7. How does the connotation of "unsinkable" add to the description of the *Titanic*?

    A It helps the reader feel the excitement on the ship.

    B It shows that people thought of the ship as invincible.

    C It shows that the ship was extremely large compared to other ships at the time.

    D It helps the reader visualize the beauty of the ship.

8. How did people's feelings about the *Titanic* affect the way they reacted to the tragedy?

    A It made people react more intensely to the crisis.

    B It made them feel this tragedy was no different than any other sinking ship.

    C It made wealthy people feel more vulnerable.

    D It made people realize that they will easily accept false security.

9. The author writes that "The legacy of the Titanic became one not only of death and loss, but of life and safety for all who sail." What does he or she mean by this?

10. According to the selection, why might things have turned out better if the sea had been rougher that night?

Read the selection below. Then read each question and choose the best answer. Use the provided answer sheet at the end of the workbook to record your answers, and use a separate sheet of paper to record your response to the open-ended question.

Dispersal and Propagation of Plants

One property of populations is dispersion, the spatial distribution of the individuals. If individual plants are too close together, they must compete with each other for available water, nutrients, and sunlight. One reason for the success of the seed plants is the development of structures that are adapted for dispersing offspring—fruits and seeds.

Fruits and seeds are dispersed by animals, wind, water, forcible discharge, and gravity. You may have walked through a field and unwittingly collected burrs, or stickers, on your shoes and socks. These burrs are fruits, and you helped disperse them. The smell, bright color, or flavor of many fruits attract animals. When animals eat such fruits, the seeds often pass unharmed through their digestive system.

Fruits and seeds dispersed by wind or water are adapted to those methods of dispersal. Orchids have tiny dust-like seeds that can easily be carried by a slight breeze. Many plants that grow near water produce fruits and seeds that contain air chambers, which allow them to float. Coconuts, for example, may float thousands of kilometers on ocean currents.

The most dramatic method of seed dispersal occurs in plants that forcibly discharge their seeds from their fruits. The tropical sandbox tree, which has fruits that hurl seeds up to 100 m (328 ft), seems to hold the distance record.

Although gymnosperms do not produce fruits, their cones may help protect seeds and aid in seed dispersal. Pine seeds are often dispersed when gravity causes cones to drop and roll away from the parent tree. Pine seeds have wings that aid in wind dispersal.

Dispersal and Propagation of Plants

1. Based on the information in the passage, the plants that had no means of dispersal would

   A create a dense forest or jungle.

   B be unable to reproduce.

   C be forced to compete for resources.

   D have overlapping root structures.

2. The title of the selection clarifies that the selection is about

   A the parts of a plant.

   B how plants propagate.

   C different types of plants.

   D how plants obtain water.

3. Which statement supports the idea that animals are an integral part of the dispersion of seeds?

   A Orchids have tiny dust-like seeds that can easily be carried by a slight breeze.

   B One property of populations is dispersion, the spatial distribution of the individuals.

   C When animals eat such fruits, the seeds often pass unharmed through their digestive system.

   D The tropical sandbox tree, which has fruits that hurl seeds up to 100 m (328 ft).

4. Based on the context of the last paragraph, a *gymnosperm* is a plant

   A whose seeds are not enclosed in fruit.

   B that reproduces asexually.

   C whose seeds are easily dispersed by wind.

   D that forcibly discharges its seeds from its fruit.

Dispersal and Propagation of Plants

5. Which is the **best** summary of this passage?

   A To avoid competition, plants have developed various methods of fruit and seed dispersal.

   B Plants often use wind and water currents to disperse seeds.

   C Tropical plants like coconuts and sandbox trees have especially aggressive dispersal methods.

   D Plants use fruits to attract animals.

6. Which statement about seed plant dispersion is an **opinion**?

   A You may have walked through a field and unwittingly collected burrs, or stickers, on your shoes and socks.

   B Many plants that grow near water produce fruits and seeds that contain air chambers, which allow them to float.

   C Although gymnosperms do not produce fruits, their cones may help protect seeds and aid in seed dispersal.

   D The most dramatic method of seed dispersal occurs in plants that forcibly discharge their seeds from their fruits.

7. Which of these passages would **most likely** be found with this selection in a collection of articles on the same topic?

   A Planting and Growing Trees

   B Proliferation of Disease in Schools

   C Plants for Food

   D Extinct Animals

8. According to the passage, what is the effect of competition among plants for water, nutrients, and sunlight?

   A Competition makes it more difficult for individual plants to survive.

   B Competition results in the extinction of plant species.

   C Competition aids in natural selection.

   D Competition causes plants to forcibly discharge their seeds.

Dispersal and Propagation of Plants

9. Which of the following changes would make the text *most* consistent in its organization?

   A Begin the selection with the last paragraph.

   B Delete the last paragraph because it does not describe dispersing fruits and seeds.

   C Begin the selection with the third paragraph.

   D Combine the last two paragraphs.

10. Explain the concept of "spatial distribution." Use the example of plants in your explanation.

Read the selection below. Then read each question and choose the best answer. Use the provided answer sheet at the end of the workbook to record your answers, and use a separate sheet of paper to record your response to open-ended questions.

Schoolwork Employment Agency

Quality Employees

Looking for someone to help with cleaning or to finish that project you started? Want it done right by people you can trust? The Schoolwork Employment Agency (SEA) can provide skilled workers for just about any job around your home. From baby-sitting to yardwork, we've got talented, eager, service-oriented young men and women who can get the job done.

SEA has been in business nationwide for five years. Our local-area office manager, Jesse Garcia, joined SEA when he was a senior in high school. Now he has a four-year college degree and is taking evening courses to earn a master's degree in business administration. Doesn't this sound like the kind of goal-oriented person you want working at your home?

All of our employees are part-time workers like Jesse, balancing their jobs with their education. What's more, they are all good students. We don't hire everyone we interview—only the candidates who impress us with their grades and their attitudes.

As an employee of SEA, anyone we send to your home will be fully insured and bonded, so you don't need to worry about accidents or other problems associated with having strangers working in your home.

Competitive Rates

In addition to providing extremely competent employees, our rates are the most reasonable in town. Compare and see how much you can save.

Convenient Service

To inquire about hiring an SEA employee, call Liz Banks at our local number, or call our toll-free 800 number for our corporate headquarters. A worker can be at your door within 24 hours. Our staff includes day students, evening students, and students on flexible schedules, so you don't have to wait for weekends or summer vacation to hire a hard-working student. We accept cash, major credit cards, and checks drawn on local banks.

Employment Opportunities

Looking for a job yourself? Are you enrolled as a student in high school, a two-year college, a four-year college, or a technical school? Do you have a good academic average and some spare time? Are you a reliable person who isn't afraid of hard work? If you answered "Yes" to all of these questions, we would like to talk to you. Call our local number and ask to speak with Carol Brown or Hal Rizzuto to schedule an interview. Be sure to bring a copy of your latest report card or college transcript.

Schoolwork Employment Agency*	Other Agencies**
Yardwork $9.75/hour	$11.00/hour
Housework $10.25/hour	$11.50/hour
Baby-sitting $6.00/hour	$7.50/hour
* Prices apply to most yardwork, housework, and baby-sitting jobs. Baby-sitting rate is based on one child. Rates for additional children and other yard or housework services are higher.	
** Based on the average of advertised rates at three different local employment agencies. Actual rates for each service vary from agency to agency.	

Schoolwork Employment Agency

1. Which of the following statements from the passage is *least* relevant to the quality of the Schoolwork Employment Agency's services?

    A   All of our employees are part-time workers like Jesse, balancing their jobs with their education.

    B   As an employee of SEA, anyone we send to your home will be fully insured and bonded, so you don't need to worry about accidents or other problems associated with having strangers working in your home.

    C   A worker can be at your door within 24 hours.

    D   We don't hire everyone we interview—only the candidates who impress us with their grades and their attitudes.

2. Someone applying for a job should bring a report card or college transcript

    A   for identification.

    B   as proof of citizenship.

    C   because the agency hires only good students.

    D   to get a student discount on the fees the agency charges.

3. The word that *best* describes the information in the last two rows of the table is

    A   indexes.

    B   price lists.

    C   disclaimers.

    D   safety warnings.

4. Based on the information in the table, which job would you expect to cost $9.75 per hour?

    A   mowing a lawn

    B   vacuuming a room

    C   caring for two children

    D   scrubbing a kitchen floor

5. What is the author saying about the employees in the section titled "Quality Employees"?

    A   They are well paid.

    B   They are reliable workers.

    C   They are creative thinkers.

    D   They are career service employees.

Schoolwork Employment Agency

6. The selection was *most likely* written for

   A corporations.

   B individual adults.

   C small offices.

   D temp agencies.

7. The *most* important effect of using a table for some of the information is to

   A fill extra space.

   B try to make the flyer look professional.

   C make up for the lack of a picture.

   D make key information stand out.

8. Based on the context of the fourth paragraph, *insured and bonded* means

   A confident and well-to-do.

   B talented and energetic.

   C experienced in buying and selling insurance.

   D covered for any financial loss they might cause.

9. Write a one-sentence summary of the last paragraph.

10. Identify five arguments the author uses and choose the one that you think is *most* persuasive. Explain the reason for your choice.

Read the editorial below. Then read each question and choose the best answer. Use the provided answer sheet at the end of the workbook to record your answers, and use a separate sheet of paper to record your response to the open-ended question.

Wanted: School Spirit

Dear Editor,

We have a big problem here at Robertson High School. It is called apathy. I see it at almost every school-sponsored event. At our last home football game against Marshall, there were more fans in attendance from Marshall—even though they had to take a thirty-minute bus ride to get here—than there were from Robertson. And most of the Robertson fans were parents of the players on the team. Of course, it was great to see the parents at the game, but where were the students who should have been cheering for the team?

At a recent band concert, I, along with the other members of the Service Club, set up more than two hundred folding chairs in the cafetorium. We needn't have bothered since fewer than fifty people attended the concert, and once again, most of them were parents.

I've talked this over with many students and teachers. I've spoken to the small handful of spirited students whom I do see at these kinds of events, and I've also talked with my classmates who pull a Houdini act the minute the dismissal bell rings. I've heard every excuse you can possibly imagine from students: "I have too much homework," "I have music lessons," "I have to go to religious school," "I must do chores." Others whine. No doubt some of these excuses are legitimate, but I can't believe that every student in the school is so diligent about homework or so overbooked every day of the week that we can't have a respectable showing at our school events.

The proof of my argument is the attendance at our baseball games for the past two seasons. The stands are always packed. The reason why is no secret. Rocky James is the best player in Robertson's history, and he's a thrill to watch. Every time he pitches, we expect a shutout if not a no-hitter; and every time he steps up to the plate, we expect a hit if not a towering home run. I am as proud of Rocky's accomplishments as everyone else, but I worry about the future and about our other school events.

What will happen next year when Rocky is a freshman in college? Will fans still come to our Robertson baseball games? And what about our other programs? If the homework, the music lessons, the dishes, and all the other excuses can wait when Rocky is pitching, why can't they sometimes take a back seat to a basketball game, a band concert, or the school play?

Speaking of the school play, it is now less than a week away from opening night, and advance ticket sales have been dismal. The play runs from Thursday through Saturday, so even those students who have a legitimate conflict or two should be able to make it to one of the performances. The cast has been working very hard for almost two months to prepare an excellent musical comedy. Let's not let them down.

If we do let the cast down, who will ultimately suffer? For how many more years can we expect to have sports teams, school plays, concerts, and other activities if so few people show up? How would you feel if you went to all the trouble of rehearsing for a show, practicing for a team, or learning to play an instrument, only to find that so few of your fellow students care to come out and support you?

I hope this letter will light a fire under the students at this school and spur them to action. If it doesn't I can picture a puzzled student body a few years from now wondering why Robertson has canceled all extracurricular activities.

Sincerely,
Dennis Elliot

Wanted: School Spirit

1. What does the word *apathy* in the passage mean?

   A tardiness

   B indifference

   C rowdiness

   D poverty

2. The letter writer is a member of the

   A baseball team.

   B basketball team.

   C Service Club.

   D Drama Club.

3. Which statement best supports the idea that lack of team support will hurt the school in the future?

   A How would you feel if you went to all the trouble of rehearsing for a show, practicing for a team, or learning to play an instrument, only to find that so few of your fellow students care to come out and support you?

   B And most of the Robertson fans were parents of the players on the team.

   C I can picture a puzzled student body a few years from now wondering why Robertson has cancelled all extracurricular activities.

   D Will fans still come to our Robertson baseball games?

4. Why does the writer use the example of the baseball games?

   A to prove that there is no school spirit at all

   B to explain why the future is dismal

   C to give people a reason to come and support other events

   D to show that people do have time to come to some things

Wanted: School Spirit

5. Which persuasive technique does the letter writer use in the fifth and seventh paragraphs?

    A asking rhetorical questions

    B appealing to readers' vanity

    C citing facts and statistics

    D begging and pleading

6. Which is a fact expressed in the letter?

    A We have a big problem here at Robertson Middle School.

    B Fewer than fifty people attended the band concert.

    C Rocky James is the best player in Robertson's history.

    D The cast has been working very hard for almost two months.

7. In this letter, what does pulling "a Houdini act" mean?

    A escaping from a locked trunk

    B escaping from handcuffs

    C pulling a rabbit from a hat

    D disappearing from sight

8. Read this sentence from the passage.

    If we do let the cast down, who will ultimately suffer?

    The underlined phrase is an example of

    A exaggeration.

    B an idiom.

    C an analogy.

    D a metaphor.

9. How might the story of the fans from Marshall be an example of faulty logic?

    A Maybe Marshall's football team has a star player.

    B There were more fans from Marshall than from Robertson.

    C Traveling to a game does not show any extra effort.

    D Some of the Marshall's fans were parents, too.

10. Do you think the writer presents the argument well? Use examples from the editorial to support your answer.

Read the selection below. Then read each question and choose the best answer. Use the provided answer sheet at the end of the workbook to record your answers, and use a separate sheet of paper to record your response to the open-ended question.

Editorial to the City

Dear Ms. James:

1   (1) Our city's parks need help. Imagine a large dog running straight at you as you peacefully stroll through your neighborhood park. (2) The dog is not on a leash, and the owner is somewhere else in the park. (3) This scene occurs every day in the park near my house so it probably happens in other parks, too. (4) Dogs that are allowed to run loose in the parks threaten people and other animals. (5) The city must pass a law that requires all dogs to be controlled on a leash in public parks.

2   (6) The city needs a leash law because dogs that run loose can injure children and leashed dogs. (7) Children play in the park and they should not have to worry that they will encounter an out-of-control dog. (8) You can never be sure if a loose dog is friendly. (9) Yesterday, a small dog and its' owner, who had her dog on a leash, were chased all the way through the park by an unleashed dog. (10) Our parks would be more safer and more fun for everyone, especially children, if dogs were required to be on leashes.

3   (11) A leash law would also protect the dogs. (12) Dogs that run loose are in danger of getting hurt if they wander into the street. (13) Dr. Winston, a veterinarian whose office is near Elmwood Park, says that in the last four months he has treated six dogs that were hit by cars near the park. (14) Dr. Winston is a great veterinarian. (15) Dog owners act irresponsibly when they do not use leashes and dogs would be safer if they were under control.

4   (16) Keeping children and other dogs safe from unleashed dogs and protecting all dogs from harm are important reasons for passing a strict leash law. (17) Please support a law that requires all dogs in our parks to be leashed. (18) Then enforce this law by having park police patrol the parks. (19) The officers should issue citations to dog owners who violate the law. (20) Make the parks safe for people and animals alike.

Sincerely,
Sandra Kim

Editorial to the City

1. Which sentence from the letter shows the *main* purpose of this selection?

   A The city must pass a law that requires all dogs to be controlled on a leash in public parks.

   B This scene occurs everyday in the park near my house so it probably happens in other parks, too.

   C A leash law would also protect the dogs.

   D Dogs that run loose are in danger of getting hurt if they wander into the street.

2. Which sentence in Paragraph 3 does *not* support the main idea of the paragraph and should be removed?

   A Sentence 11

   B Sentence 12

   C Sentence 14

   D Sentence 15

3. Which tactic could *best* support the idea that dogs running loose can injure children?

   A discussing how leashes affect dogs

   B explaining how children run from strange dogs

   C supplying an example of children being chased by loose dogs

   D listing how many unleashed dogs have been seen in the park

4. What stage of the writing process is represented by the web below?

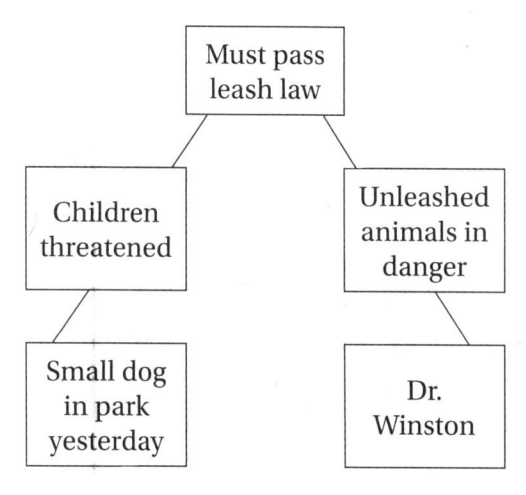

   A editing

   B revision

   C publishing

   D prewriting

Editorial to the City

5. Read Sentence 12 and Sentence 13 of the third paragraph.

   Which transitional word or phrase would best fit at the beginning of the second sentence?

   A   In fact,

   B   That is,

   C   However,

   D   Nevertheless,

6. With which statement would the writer of the letter *disagree*?

   A   People should love all animals.

   B   All animals were meant to roam free.

   C   Veterinarians care about the safety of animals.

   D   Children deserve to feel safe in city parks.

7. According to the selection, how would a leash law protect dogs?

   A   It would keep small dogs safe from being stolen by children who want to take them home.

   B   It would keep dogs from being picked up by dog catchers.

   C   It would keep dogs from eating trash and getting sick.

   D   It would keep small dogs safe from large dogs that might chase them.

8. What implied question does Sandra Kim answer for Mrs. James?

   A   Why do we need a leash law?

   B   Should we allow dogs in parks?

   C   When is it safe for children to pet dogs?

   D   How can dog owners be more responsible?

Editorial to the City

9. What is *most likely* the reason Sandra Kim describes the park near her home?

   A She wants the laws changed at her park first.

   B She is a dog-watcher.

   C She does not know about any other parks.

   D She wants to show she has personal knowledge of the situation.

10. What do you see as the most persuasive argument the author uses in favor of a leash law for dogs?

Read the poems below. Then read each question and choose the best answer. Use the provided answer sheet at the end of the workbook to record your answers, and use a separate sheet of paper to record your responses to the open-ended questions.

The Wind
by James Stephens

The wind stood up, and gave a shout;
He whistled on his fingers, and

Kicked the withered leaves about,
And thumped the branches with his hand,

And said he'd kill, and kill, and kill;
And so he will! And so he will!

The Wind Tapped Like a Tired Man
by Emily Dickinson

The wind tapped like a tired man,
And like a host, "Come in,"
I boldly answered; entered then
My residence within

A rapid, footless guest,
To offer whom a chair
Were as impossible as hand
A sofa to the air.

No bone had he to bind him,
His speech was like the push
Of numerous hummingbirds at once
From a superior bush.

His countenance[1] a billow,
His fingers, if he pass,
Let go a music, as of tunes
Blown tremulous[2] in glass.

He visited, still flitting;
Then, like a timid man,
Again he tapped—'twas flurriedly[3]—
And I became alone.

---

1. **countenance:** face, expression
2. **tremulous:** vibrating, quivering
3. **flurriedly:** excitedly

The Wind / The Wind Tapped Like a Tired Man

1. Stephens' poem takes place in what season?

   A   winter

   B   spring

   C   summer

   D   fall

2. In "The Wind," Stephens *mainly* uses

   A   personification.

   B   alliteration.

   C   allegory.

   D   irony.

3. Which word *best* describes the mood of Emily Dickinson's poem?

   A   excited

   B   lonely

   C   mourning

   D   fearful

4. Which line from Dickinson's poem *best* supports the conclusion that the wind blew gently?

   A   A rapid, footless guest,

   B   No bone had he to bind him,

   C   His fingers, if he pass,

   D   He visited, still flitting;

5. A ballad about this same topic would *most likely*

   A   tell a story about someone's experience with the wind.

   B   rhyme and have just 14 lines.

   C   praise all of nature, especially the wind.

   D   mourn someone's death and describe a windy funeral.

6. In Dickinson's poem, she compares the wind to

   A   a sofa.

   B   a person without legs.

   C   the air.

   D   a hand.

The Wind / The Wind Tapped Like a Tired Man

7. James Stephens' poem is written in the

   A first person.

   B second person.

   C third person.

   D first and second person.

8. Give an example of a simile and then analyze how the use of similes enhances the meaning of "The wind tapped like a tired man."

9. What real-life experience is Stephens describing in "The Wind"?

10. Both of these poems describe the wind. Compare and contrast these two poems and their views.

Writing Test Practice

Writing Test Practice And The Indiana Statewide Testing For Educational Progress-Plus (ISTEP+) Test

The Grade 9 *ISTEP+* English/Language Arts Test

In grade nine you will take the Writing Test portion of the *ISTEP+*. This test is composed of two sections.

In the Language Conventions section of the ISTEP+, you will be presented with ten multiple-choice questions that will assess your abilities to use paragraphing, grammar, usage, spelling, punctuation, and capitalization.

In the Writing Applications section of the *ISTEP+*, you will be asked to compose a response to a narrative, informational, descriptive, or persuasive prompt: Your response will require a well-developed and well-organized presentation of ideas that follow a particular format suitable to the purpose and audience. You will be expected to develop your written response by following the steps in the writing process: prewriting, drafting, revising, editing, and producing a final copy. Your response will be scored on both content and conventions.

Your content score will be based on the following six-point rubric:

SCORE OF 6
Ideas & Content Unifying theme, completely focused on the topic, with in-depth information and exceptional supporting details.

Organization Meaningful, cohesive whole with a beginning, middle, and end; progresses in a way that enhances meaning, with smooth transitions between ideas, sentences, and paragraphs.

Style Challenging vocabulary with detailed and precise explanations, rich descriptions, and clear, vivid actions. Writing is exceptionally fluent, with varied sentence patterns, and uses writing techniques such as imagery and dialogue.

Voice Appropriate register to suit the task, a strong sense of audience, and an original perspective.

SCORE OF 5
Ideas & Content Unifying theme, focused on the topic, with in-depth information and supporting details.

Organization Meaningful, cohesive whole with a beginning, middle, and end; progresses in a way that enhances meaning, with smooth transitions between sentences and paragraphs.

Style Controlled vocabulary with detailed and precise explanations, rich descriptions, and clear, vivid actions. Writing is very fluent, with varied sentence patterns, and uses writing techniques such as imagery and dialogue.

Voice Appropriate register to suit the task, a strong sense of audience, and an original perspective.

SCORE OF 4
Ideas & Content Unifying theme, mostly focused on the topic, with sufficient information; supporting details may not be fully developed.

Organization Meaningful whole with a beginning, middle, and end, despite an occasional lapse; generally progresses in a way that enhances meaning, with transitions between sentences and paragraphs; some topic sentences are included.

Style Basic vocabulary with words that clearly convey the writer's meaning. Writing is fluent, with some varied sentence patterns, and attempts to use writing techniques such as imagery and dialogue.

Voice Appropriate register to suit the task, some sense of audience; attempts an original perspective.

SCORE OF 3
Ideas & Content Unifying theme attempted, somewhat focused on the topic; includes some information and a few details.

Organization Weak or absent beginning, middle, and end; attempts to progress in a way that enhances meaning; attempts transitions between sentences and paragraphs.

Style Basic vocabulary with predictable and common words. Writing is generally fluent, with mostly simple sentences that are ordinary and predictable.

Voice Difficulty in establishing a register, with little sense of audience, and lacking an original perspective.

SCORE OF 2
Ideas & Content Attempts a main idea, but sometimes loses focus; little information is included with few or no details.

Organization Has only one or two of the three elements (beginning, middle, and end), is sometimes difficult to follow, with weak or absent transitions.

Style Limited vocabulary; writing exhibits some fluency but is often repetitive, predictable, or dull, relying mostly on simple sentences.

Voice Register inappropriate to the task, little or no sense of audience, and lacking an original perspective.

SCORE OF 1
Ideas & Content Difficult for the reader to discern the main idea; too brief or too repetitive to establish a focus, with little information and few details.

Organization Has only one or two of the three elements (beginning, middle, and end), is difficult to follow, with weak or absent transitions and no topic sentences.

Style Limited vocabulary, with many incorrect words. Writing is flat, lifeless, and has problems with sentence patterns.

Voice Difficulty in choosing an appropriate register, with no sense of audience, and no original perspective.

Your conventions score will be based on the following four-point rubric:

SCORE OF 4
Very few or no errors in capitalization, punctuation, spelling, grammar, word usage, paragraphing; very few or no run-on sentences or sentence fragments; errors do not impair the flow of communication.

SCORE OF 3
Occasional errors in capitalization, punctuation, spelling, grammar, word usage, paragraphing; may have run-on sentences or sentence fragments; errors do not seriously obscure the writer's meaning.

SCORE OF 2
Frequent errors in capitalization, punctuation, spelling, grammar, word usage; paragraphing may be missing; run-on sentences or sentence fragments are likely; errors will impair communication, but with a little extra effort on the reader's part, it is still possible to discern most, if not all, of what the writer is trying to communicate.

SCORE OF 1
Many errors in capitalization, punctuation, spelling, grammar, word usage; paragraphing may be missing; run-on sentences or sentence fragments are likely; errors cause the reader to struggle to discern the writer's meaning, and may make it impossible to ascertain what the writer is attempting to communicate.

Writing Test Practice

On the following pages you will find the writing test practice section: questions and writing prompts like those on your Indiana writing test. These prompts address the skills and standards that you are expected to master. Preceding these prompts are writing strategies and tips that you can use to help you be successful on your state test.

TIPS FOR STUDENTS: WRITING

The primary goal of the practice in this Writing section is to help you prepare for the *ISTEP+*, *ISTEP+* GQE Grade 9 Writing Test. In order to write a concise response, you must learn to organize your thoughts before you begin writing the actual response. This keeps you from straying too far from the prompt's topic.

Strategies for Responding to a Prompt

- First, **read the prompt carefully.** Be sure that you understand exactly what the prompt is asking.

- **Decide what kind of response you are being asked to write.** You will be asked to write narrative, informational, descriptive and persuasive responses. **You should ask yourself, "What is the purpose of this response?"** For example, are you writing a cause-and-effect response, or a definition response? When you understand the type of response you are being asked to write, you will have a sense of the purpose of your response.

- Next, **organize your thoughts.** It is best to write down notes on a separate piece of paper before actually writing the response. First, determine the main point of your response. Your topic sentence should include the general topic as well as the main idea. It should set the tone and catch the reader's attention. Most importantly, make sure it is answering the prompt. This will be the anchor to your response. Then, come up with ideas to support your topic sentence. Your ideas should include the major points that you want to cover in your response.

- Write in complete sentences, and be aware of unity within the response. In other words, make sure your sentences and paragraphs "flow" smoothly. Sentences should come together smoothly to support the main idea and should be arranged in an order that makes sense to the reader. Be as specific as possible when stating your ideas. Make use of transitional words or phrases if necessary. Also, remember to write neatly.

- Finally, **proofread your response.** Check for spelling and punctuation errors. Look for run-on sentences and sentence fragments. Look over verb tenses to see if you have used them correctly. Make the necessary edits as neat as possible.

If you follow the above guidelines, you should succeed on the writing section of standardized tests. Remember that practice makes perfect. Read and write as often as possible on whatever subjects you prefer, and you will see that writing responses will eventually come quite naturally.

When It's Test Time...

Here are some final tips for test day.

- Be sure that you are well rested.
- Be on time, and be sure that you have the necessary materials.
- Listen to the instructions of the teacher.
- Read directions and questions carefully.
- Remain calm and remember what you have learned in class, and you should do well.

Good luck!

GRAPHIC ORGANIZERS FOR WRITING

Brainstorming Significant Details

You might like to start by noting significant details in a word web. Write your topic in the middle circle. Then write words or phrases that come to mind in the outer circles.

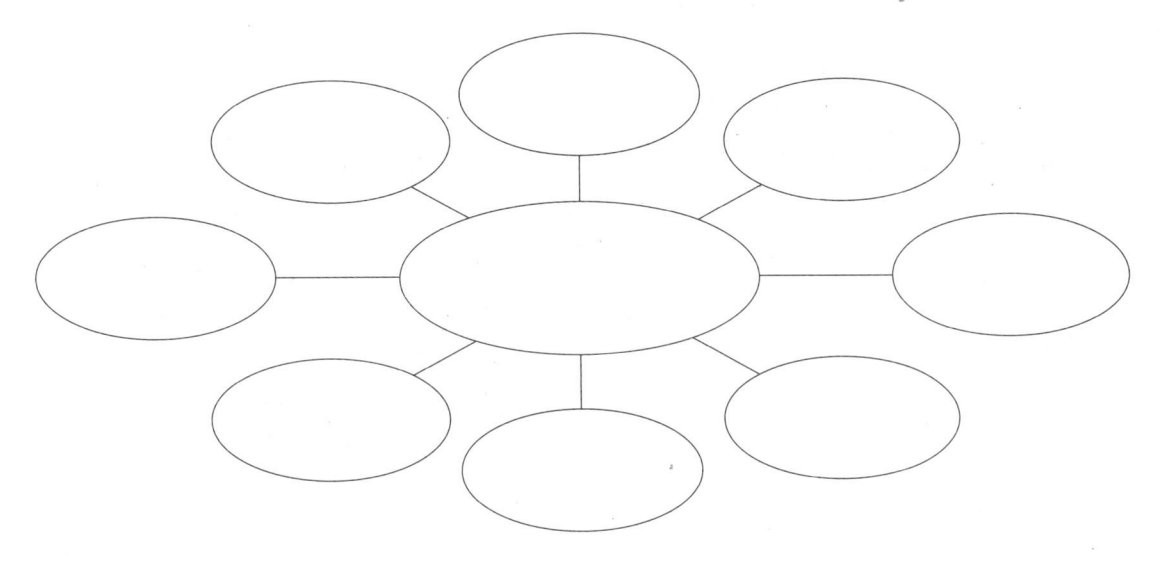

Definition Map

The tool below can be used to brainstorm an extended definition.

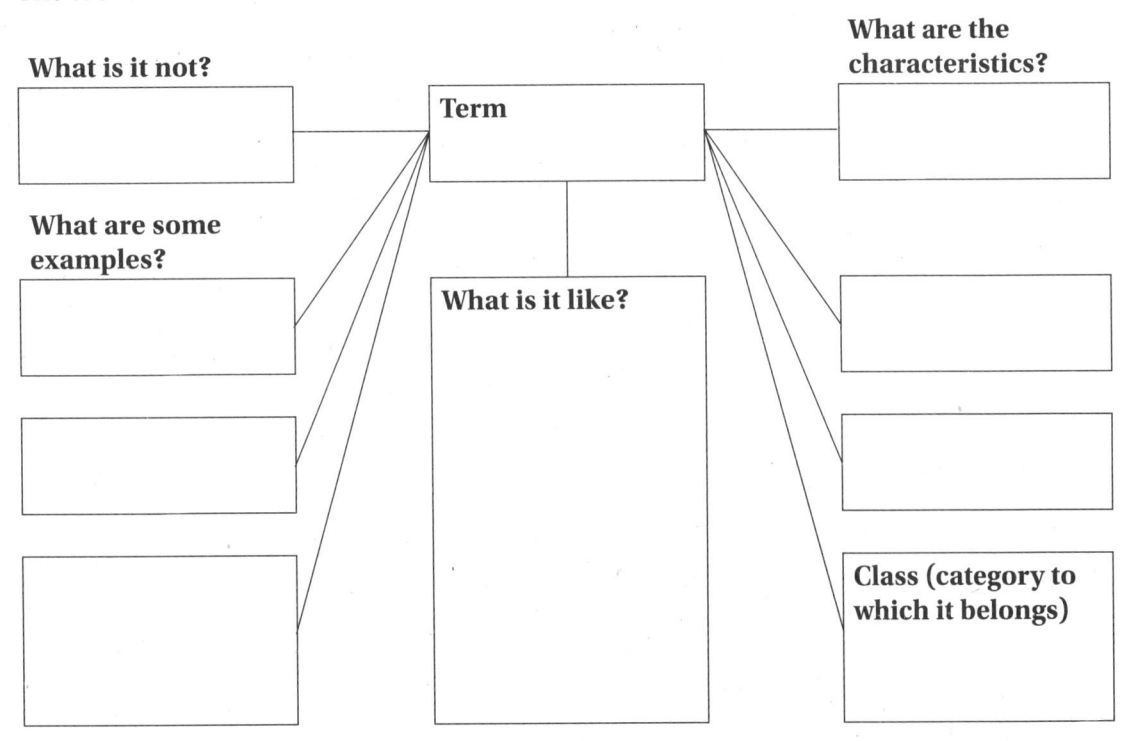

What is it not?

What are the characteristics?

Term

What are some examples?

What is it like?

Class (category to which it belongs)

71

GRAPHIC ORGANIZERS FOR WRITING

Compare & Contrast

To compare and contrast information, use a Venn diagram like the one below to organize your information. Note differences in the outer circles and similarities where the circles overlap.

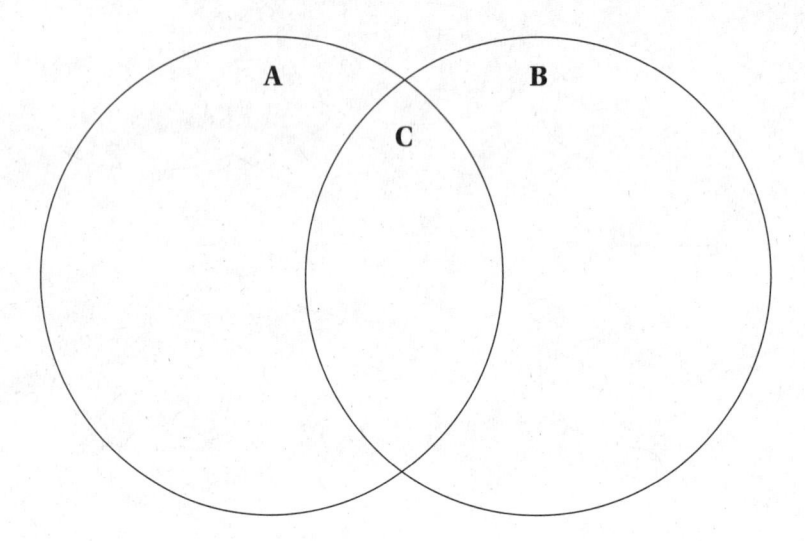

A   B
C

Persuasion

If you need to persuade your reader, you might want to use this organizer. Write your opinion in the arrow at the top. Then list convincing reasons and supporting details.

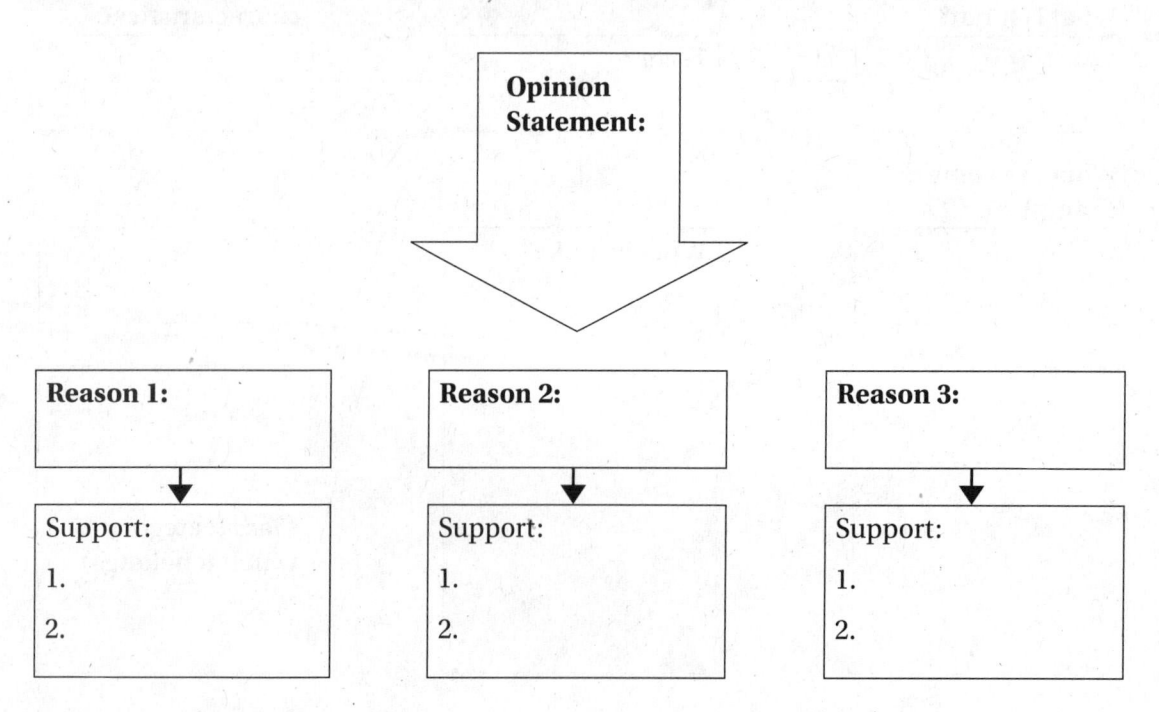

Opinion Statement:

Reason 1:

Support:
1.
2.

Reason 2:

Support:
1.
2.

Reason 3:

Support:
1.
2.

GRAPHIC ORGANIZERS FOR WRITING

Develop a Thesis

Use the graphic organizer below to develop a thesis. If the prompt calls for an explanation of causes only, then ignore the "Effects" boxes.

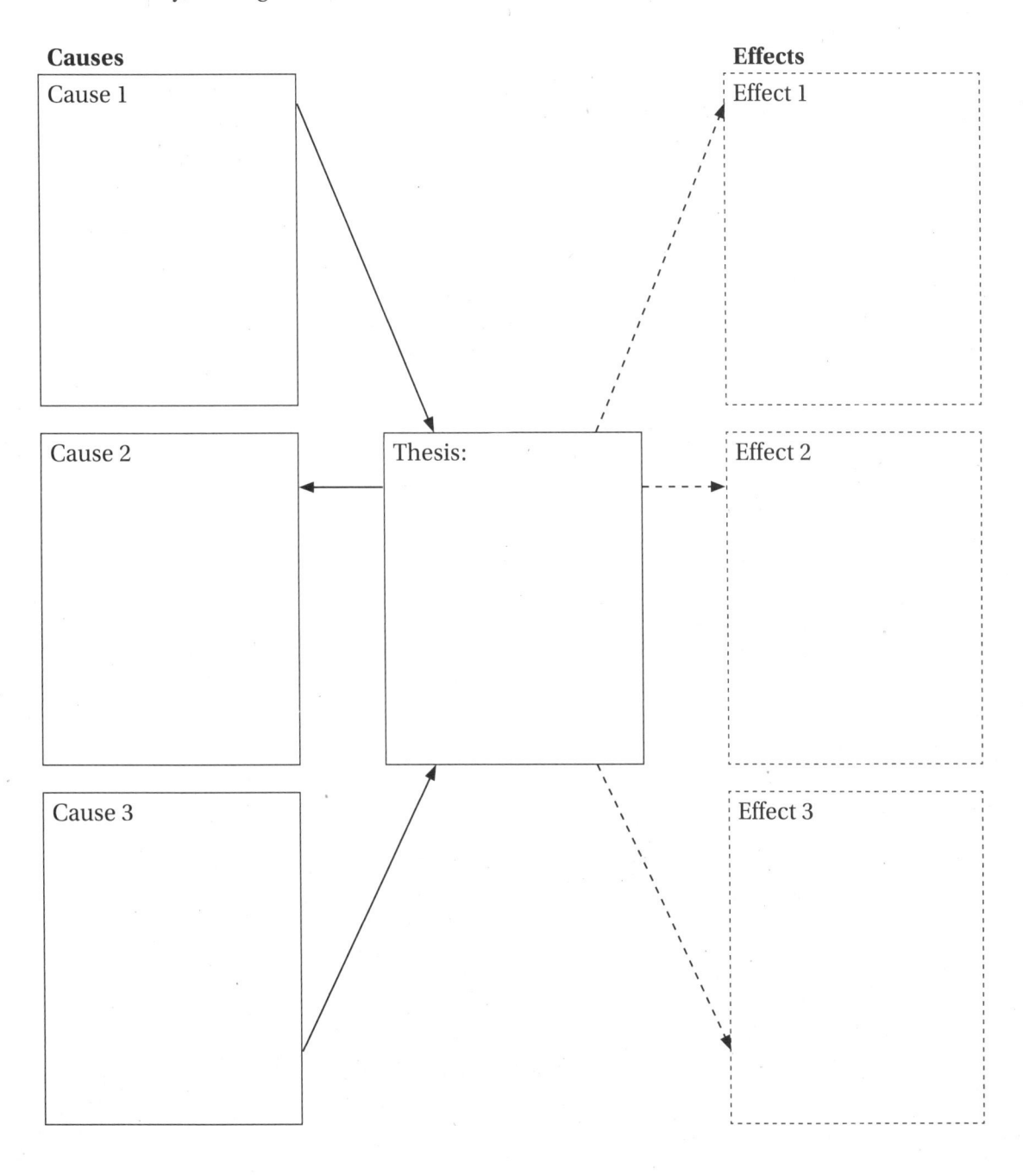

Causes
- Cause 1
- Cause 2
- Cause 3

Thesis:

Effects
- Effect 1
- Effect 2
- Effect 3

Writing Prompt 1

Plan, write, and proofread a persuasive essay in response to the writing prompt below.

> Your local school board is discussing the possibility of requiring school uniforms beginning next year. They have invited people to submit their ideas on the issue in writing before the next board meeting. You decide to submit your opinion. Choose one side of the issue and write a persuasive essay.

As you write your essay, be sure to

- Focus on the positive or negative aspects of wearing uniforms.
- Think about your audience and purpose.
- Organize your response logically.
- Include relevant details to support the opinion you choose to promote.
- Edit your response to correct errors in grammar, spelling, and punctuation.

ISTEP+ Writing Applications   Grades 6–12

Score Level	Ideas and Content Does the writing sample:	Organization Does the writing sample:	Style Does the writing sample:	Voice Does the writing sample:
6	Fully accomplish the task? Include thorough, relevant, and complete ideas?	Organize ideas logically?	Exhibit exceptional word usage? Demonstrate exceptional writing technique?	Demonstrate effective adjustment of language and tone to task and reader?
5	Fully accomplish the task? Include many relevant ideas?	Organize ideas logically?	Exhibit very good word usage? Demonstrate very good writing technique?	Demonstrate effective adjustment of language and tone to task and reader?
4	Accomplish the task? Include relevant ideas?	Organize ideas logically?	Exhibit good word usage? Demonstrate good writing technique?	Demonstrate an attempt to adjust language and tone to task and reader?
3	Minimally accomplish the task? Include some relevant ideas?	Exhibit an attempt to organize ideas logically?	Exhibit ordinary word usage? Demonstrate average writing?	Demonstrate an attempt to adjust language and tone to task and reader?
2	Only partially accomplish the task? Include few relevant ideas?	Exhibit a minimal attempt to organize ideas logically?	Exhibit minimal word usage? Demonstrate minimal writing technique?	Demonstrate language and tone that may be inappropriate to task and reader?
1	Fail to accomplish the task? Include very few relevant ideas?	Organize ideas logically?	Exhibit less than minimal word usage? Demonstrate less than minimal writing technique?	Demonstrate language and tone that may be inappropriate to task and reader?

STRATEGY FOR RESPONDING TO THE PROMPT

Prewriting

1. Analyze the Prompt. Read the prompt carefully to identify the purpose of and the audience for your response.

Purpose. In the prompt above, certain clue words reveal your purpose: "... submit your opinion" and "Choose one side of the issue...." The words "Choose one side" are clues that you are to write to persuade readers to agree with your opinion. Decide whether you want to argue for or against school uniforms. Then complete the following sentence:

The purpose of this essay is to persuade _____ to _____ .

Audience. According to the prompt, who is your audience? Use the following step-by-step method to analyze the audience identified in the prompt:

Steps	Explanation	Your Response
Step 1 Ask yourself, "Who is the audience for this response?"	Look to the prompt for clues about your audience.	
Step 2 Ask, "What does my audience already know about this situation? What do they need to know?"	Put yourself in your audience's shoes and imagine what type of opinions they already have. Since they are discussing the issue, some of them may already have opinions. However, you may be able to present new information that can sway them.	
Step 3 Ask, "How can I interest my audience in the response I am going to compose?"	Remember that your audience is going to be looking for information that is delivered in a reasonable way. Put serious effort into brainstorming good ideas, and then present your opinion in a way that supports the best interest of local families and students.	

Copyright © by Holt, Rinehart and Winston. All rights reserved.

2. Develop A Thesis. Brainstorm different positive and/or negative effects of wearing school uniforms. Write these in the appropriate boxes of the graphic organizer below. Add boxes as needed. Study the different effects. Are they mostly positive or negative? Write a thesis statement that states your position on school uniforms.

If you listed mostly negative effects, then your thesis will probably be against school uniforms. In the same way, if you listed mostly positive effects, your thesis will probably be for school uniforms.

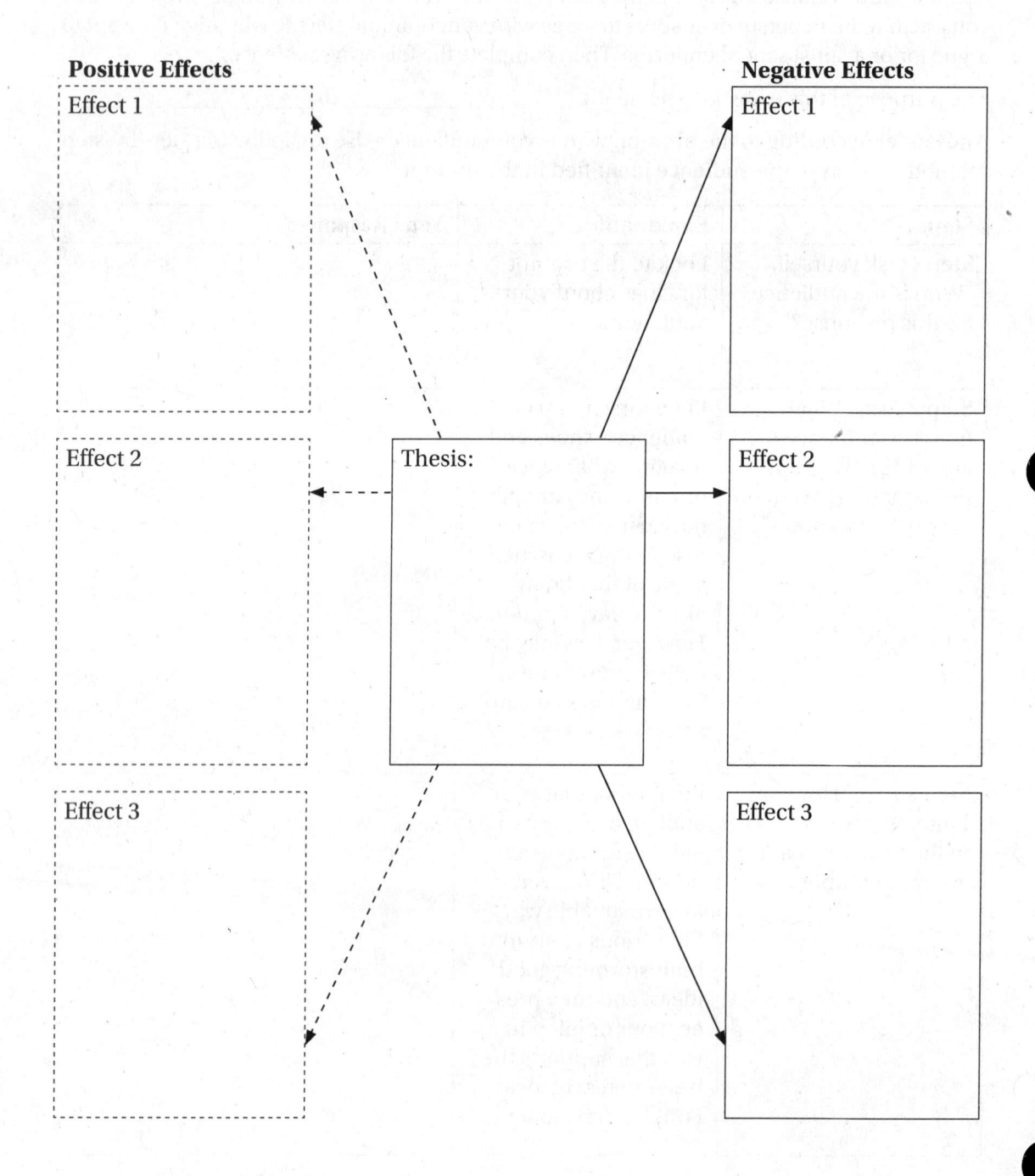

Positive Effects

Effect 1

Effect 2

Effect 3

Thesis:

Negative Effects

Effect 1

Effect 2

Effect 3

3. Gather Support. To make your response convincing, you need to include your support—examples, facts, and statistics. In a testing situation, you can use the following sources for support:

- the information provided in the prompt
- information based on your own experiences, observations, and reading

Use the graphic organizer below to collect and organize your support. Use only the parts of the chart that you need based on the requirements of the writing prompt.

Write your thesis in the arrow. Then write different reasons in the boxes. You may use the effects from the graphic organizer on the previous page. Or you may write different reasons. Finally, add supporting details for each reason.

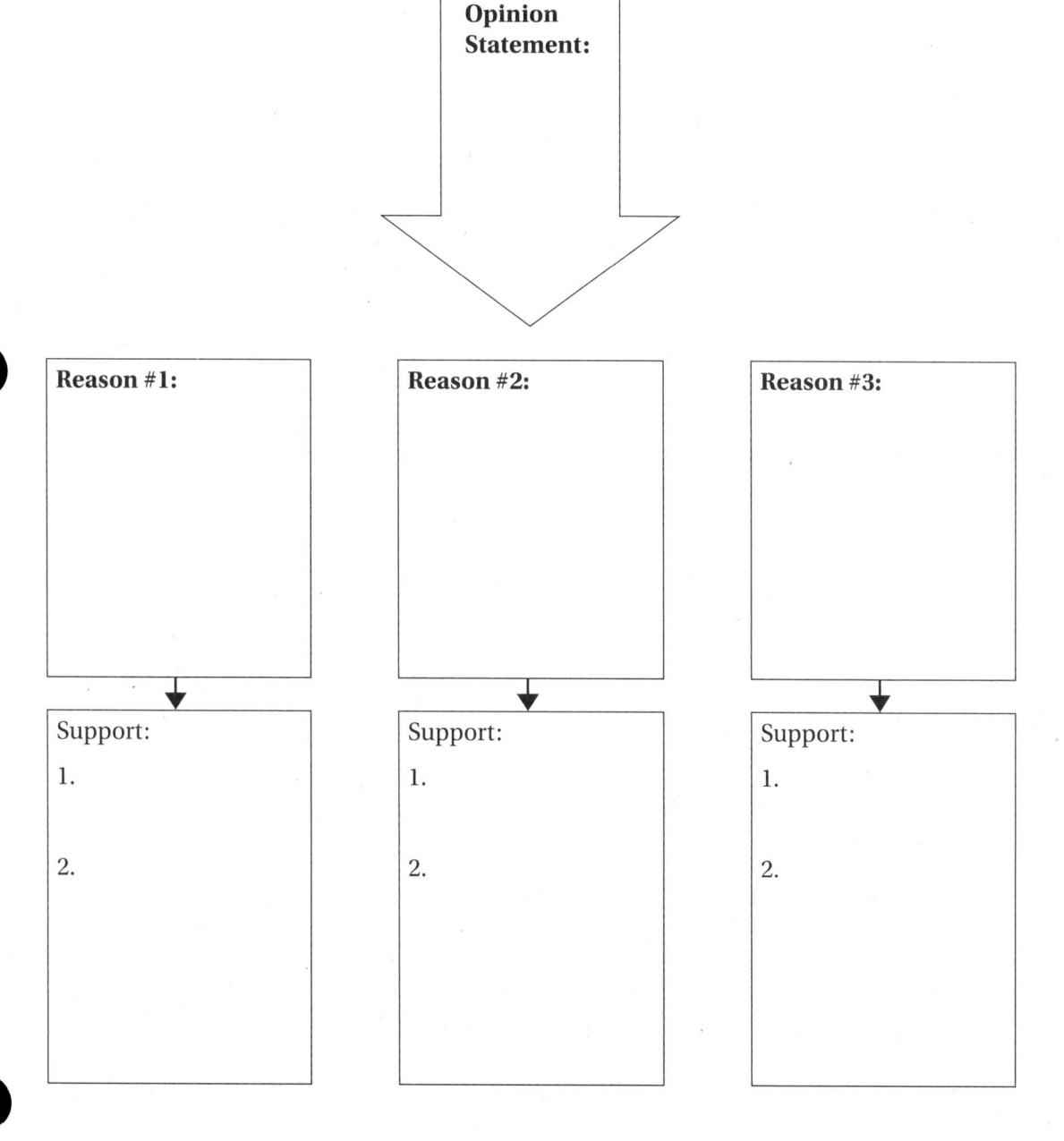

Opinion Statement:

Reason #1:

Reason #2:

Reason #3:

Support:
1.
2.

Support:
1.
2.

Support:
1.
2.

Copyright © by Holt, Rinehart and Winston. All rights reserved.

77

Drafting Your Response

Use the following framework to draft your response to the writing prompt. Write your draft on the lined pages that follow.

Framework	Directions and Explanations
Introduction	
• Attract the readers' interest. • Establish the situation or topic. • Present the thesis.	**Get your reader's respect** School board members experience a lot of negative feedback from parents and students in the district. Start off on a positive note so they do not see you as another angry person. **Get to the point** Let readers know right away why you are writing this essay. If the readers know your purpose, it will be easier for them to follow along. **State your thesis** In this case, your thesis is also your opinion. Make it clear which side of the issue you support.
Body	
• State your first reason and support with evidence. • State your second reason, and so on.	**Organize clearly** Make sure your argument progresses in a logical order. Since you are making an argument and you want to pique readers' interest right away, lead off with your most convincing information. **Support your ideas** For each aspect of school uniforms you choose to discuss, present a logical reason that supports your opinion. Use facts, examples, statistics, quotations, anecdotes or expert opinions as evidence.
Conclusion	
• Reinforce the thesis. • Tie the ideas together with a summary.	**Finish strongly** Restate your opinion and summarize your reasons. You might end by noting that others agree with your opinion and then back up the statement.

Draft your response in the space below.

Evaluating, Revising, and Editing Your Response

Use the following strategies to revise your response. You may make your revisions directly on your first draft, or, if necessary, write your revised draft on the lined pages that follow.

Evaluation Guidelines for Persuasive Response		
Evaluation Question	**Tips**	**Revision Techniques**
1. Does the response have a clear thesis? Does the thesis address the prompt?	Ask yourself, "Does my thesis clearly state my opinion?"	If necessary, **revise** your thesis to address the prompt accurately.
2. Does the response use specific details to support the reasons?	Place a dot next to each example, illustration, or anecdote.	**Elaborate** on the thesis by adding details.
3. Do the supporting details clearly relate to the reasons they are meant to support?	Lightly circle each dot that represents a relevant detail.	**Cut** supporting details that do not relate to specific reasons.
4. Are ideas logically related to one another? Are there gaps in logic or information?	Study the flow from one sentence to the next. Does each idea follow logically from the one before it?	**Add** details to fill in gaps in logic. **Add** transitions to improve the flow of ideas.
5. Does the response use appropriate, precise vocabulary?	Review your response for tired, dull vocabulary—words like *thing, very, great, bad,* and so on.	**Replace** dull, tired words with more precise, vivid language.
6. Does the response use a variety of sentence beginnings?	Place a check next to sentences beginning with a noun. If your checks are next to most sentences, revise a few.	**Rearrange** sentences so that some begin with phrases, subordinate clauses, or transitional expressions.

Draft your revised response in the space below.

Proofing Your Response

Final Editing Guidelines

Proofread your response to ensure that it

- contains only complete sentences, no fragments.
- shows proper subject-verb agreement, consistent verb tense, and correct use of nominative and subjective case.
- uses correct capitalization, punctuation, and spelling.

Draft your final response in the space below.

Writing Prompt 2

Plan, write, and proofread a narrative in response to the writing prompt below.

There are many different types of holidays. Some holidays have patriotic or political significance. Others have a religious meaning. The text below names a few of the types of holidays.

> Patriotic/political holidays are those that celebrate something or someone important to the history of a nation. Some examples in the United States are Independence Day, Martin Luther King Day, and Memorial Day.
>
> Religious holidays tend to celebrate or commemorate an event or person. A few examples of these are Christmas, Passover, and Ramadan.
>
> There are also holidays which don't quite fit into the categories described above. Examples of these are Valentine's Day and Halloween. Originally, these two holidays were religious holidays. Today, however, most people celebrate them in an entirely different manner.

Think back to the best holiday celebration you ever had. You may use one of the holidays listed above, or you may choose another one. Write a narrative about that day. Describe the people you were with, the things that you did, and what made it the best holiday ever. Be sure to use details that bring your reader to the scene—providing sights, sounds, smells, tastes, and feelings.

As you write your narrative, be sure to

- Identify the holiday.
- Tell a story, from beginning to end.
- Include plenty of details about the people you were with and what you did.
- Use transitional words and phrases to connect events and ideas.
- Organize your response so that your ideas progress logically.
- Proofread your narrative for standard grammar, usage, spelling, and punctuation.

STRATEGY FOR RESPONDING TO THE PROMPT

Prewriting

1. Analyze the Prompt. Read the prompt carefully to identify the purpose of and the audience for your response.

Purpose. In the prompt above, certain clue words reveal your purpose: "write a narrative . . . describe the people you were with . . . ." The words *narrative* and *describe* are clues that you are to write a descriptive narrative. Reread the prompt to determine what you are supposed to do in your narrative.

Complete the following sentence:

The purpose of this essay is to write a _____ describing _____ .

Audience. In this writing prompt, the audience is not named specifically. You will need to think about what audience would read a such a narrative. Use the following step-by-step method to analyze how to address your audience.

Steps	Explanation	Your Response
Step 1 Ask yourself, "Who is the audience for this response?"	Look to the prompt for clues about your audience.	
Step 2 Ask, "What does my audience already know about this holiday? What do they need to know?"	Put yourself in your audience's shoes and imagine what type of information they already have about this holiday. Even if it is a well-known holiday, your audience may not know about your personal or family traditions surrounding that day. You will need to give background information or explanations.	
Step 3 Ask, "How can I make sure to write this as a narrative?"	Remember that a narrative tells a story. It has a clear plot and sequence of events. Think about what happened that day, from the time you woke up until the time you went to bed.	

2. Develop a Thesis. While a narrative does not necessarily always have a thesis, this writing prompt asks a question that requires one. You will need to formulate a thesis statement about what made this holiday better than any other. This statement should not be written in your narrative, but your story should support this thesis. For example, a thesis might be, "This holiday was the best because all of my family were together." The narrative would then describe all of the different people who were together and show that each one was special in some way. Write your thesis in the center oval of the graphic organizer below. Then add the details that made this celebration so special. Include the setting, people, and events.

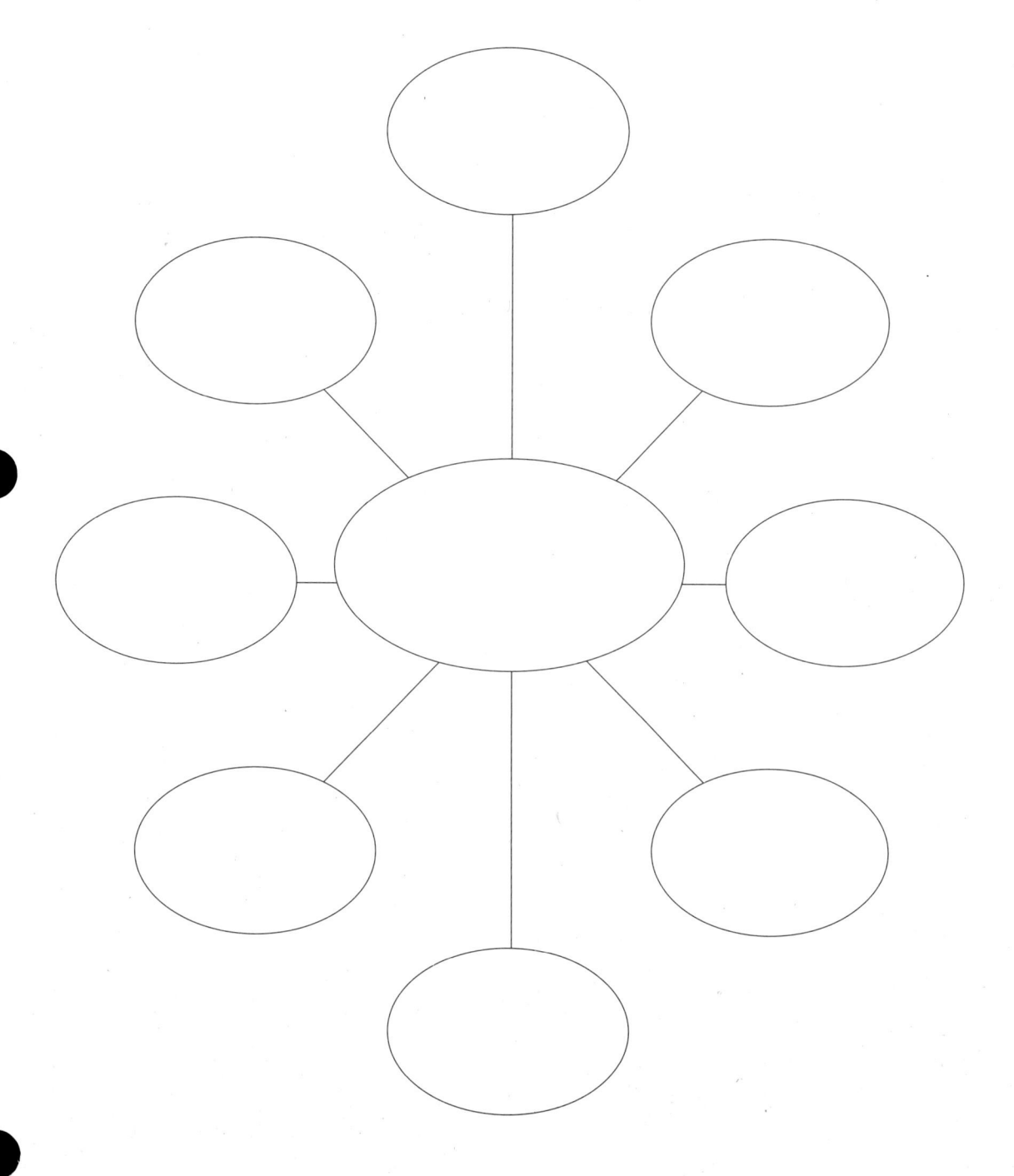

3. Organize Your Narrative. Now that you have brainstormed different details about the day, you can begin to list events and order them chronologically. Use the graphic organizer below to write different events from that day. Write a number in the Order box to show the order in which the events occurred. This will help you write the story in sequence.

Event	Order

Drafting Your Response

Use the following framework to draft your response to the writing prompt. Write your draft on the lined page that follows.

Framework	Directions and Explanations
Introduction	
• Use an attention grabber.	**Get your reader interested** Begin the story with dialogue or some other hook that will make the reader want to read on.
Body	
• Describe the setting. • Develop the plot. • Fully describe the people in the story.	**Give the time and place** Describe where and when the narrative takes place. Use details to help the reader visualize the scene. **Let the events unfold** Tell what happens. Use dialogue for people's words. **Develop the characters** This narrative's characters are the real people you were with on that day. Describe the people by telling about more than just their appearance. Use descriptive sentences and tell about their actions and words, too.
Conclusion	
• Resolve the story.	**Include a resolution** Bring the story to a close by describing how the day ended. You may describe your feelings to help the reader understand or infer your thesis.

Draft your response in the space below.

Evaluating, Revising, and Editing Your Response

Use the following strategies to evaluate and revise your response. You may make your revisions directly on your first draft, or, if necessary, write your revised draft on the lined pages that follow.

Evaluation Guidelines for Narrative Response		
Evaluation Question	**Tips**	**Revision Techniques**
1. Does the response have a clear purpose? The narrative should focus on telling the events of your best holiday celebration.	Ask yourself, "What is the narrative really about?" Be sure you can answer this question in one or two sentences.	**Review** your opening paragraph. Does it catch the reader's attention as well as introduce who or what the narrative will be about?
2. Is the response organized appropriately, to reflect the purpose?	Review your narrative and make sure the events are listed in a logical order.	**Rearrange** any events that are not in a logical order. Use transition words such as *then, next,* and *finally*.
3. Does the narrative clearly describe the setting?	Look for events that relate to where and when the story took place. Ask yourself, "Can the reader experience this setting with more than one sense?"	If necessary, **elaborate** your descriptions of the setting. Use descriptions that appeal to different senses (sight, sound, touch, smell, taste).
4. Does the narrative fully describe the people?	Ask yourself, "What other questions might a reader have about any of these people?"	**Add** details or descriptions as needed.
5. Does the response use appropriate, precise vocabulary?	Identify words that represent a stretch for you. If you are not certain of the word's meaning, revise.	**Replace** words that you are uncertain about with words that are more familiar.
6. Does the response use a variety of sentence structures?	Identify at least 1 compound sentence (2 main clauses) and 1 complex (1 independent + 1 dependent clause) per paragraph.	**Combine** ideas to create compound or complex sentences.

Draft your revised response in the space below.

Proofing Your Response

Final Editing Guidelines

Proofread your response to ensure that it

- contains only complete sentences, no fragments.
- shows proper subject-verb agreement, consistent verb tense, and correct use of nominative and subjective case.
- uses correct capitalization, punctuation, and spelling.

Draft your final response in the space below.

WRITING PROMPT 3

Plan, write, and proofread an expository essay in response to the writing prompt below. Read the following quotations about family.

> **family** *n.* **1:** a group of people living under one roof: HOUSEHOLD **2:** a group of individuals who share a common ancestor **3:** a group of people sharing the same beliefs or convictions: FELLOWSHIP **4:** a basic unit of society consisting of a parent or parents and a child or children.
>
> The Family is the Country of the heart. . . .The only pure joys unmixed with sadness which it is given to man to taste upon earth are . . . the joys of the Family.
> *Giuseppe Mazzini*
>
> Though a family be a thousand, there can be only one in charge.   *Chinese proverb*
>
> Family jokes, though rightly cursed by strangers, are the bond that keeps most families alive.   *Stella Benson*
>
> All happy families resemble one another, but each unhappy family is unhappy in its own way.   *Leo Tolstoy*
>
> I am the family face; / Flesh perishes, I live on, / Projecting trait and trace / Through time to times anon / And leaping from place to place / Over oblivion.   *Thomas Hardy*

Not all families look the same. Write an expository essay for your social studies class defining what makes a family.

As you write your essay, remember to

- Focus on the meaning of *family*.
- Consider the audience, purpose, and occasion for your response.
- Organize your response so that your ideas progress logically.
- Include relevant ideas, anecdotes, and quotations to support your definition. You may refer to, and elaborate on, one or more of the quotations above.
- Proofread your response to correct errors in grammar, spelling, and punctuation.

Strategy for Responding to the Prompt

Prewriting

1. Analyze the Prompt. Read the prompt carefully to identify the purpose of and the audience for your response.

Purpose. In the prompt, you are asked to explain the meaning of a concept—in other words, to define something. The prompt also tells you what the format for this definition is, whether it is an essay, a newspaper article, a speech, or something else.

Complete the following sentence:

The purpose of this essay is to write a _____ explaining _____ .

Audience. According to the prompt, who is your audience? Use the following step-by-step method to analyze the audience identified in the prompt.

Steps	Explanation	Your Response
Step 1 Ask yourself, "Who is the audience for this definition?"	Look to the prompt for clues about your audience.	
Step 2 Ask, "What does my audience already know about this term? What do they need to know?"	Chances are, on a test, the term will be a common one. Your challenge, then, will be to explain it in an uncommon way. Think about how you can make your audience understand something new about the concept.	
Step 3 Ask, "Does my audience already have a different definition in mind?"	Remember that your audience may expect you to discuss the term in the way they are used to understanding it. Be sure to acknowledge what they already think of when they hear the term.	

2. Define Your Term. This writing prompt gave you a dictionary definition and several different people's ideas about the term. You can use these ideas as a springboard for your essay. Use the definition map below to brainstorm your extended definition.

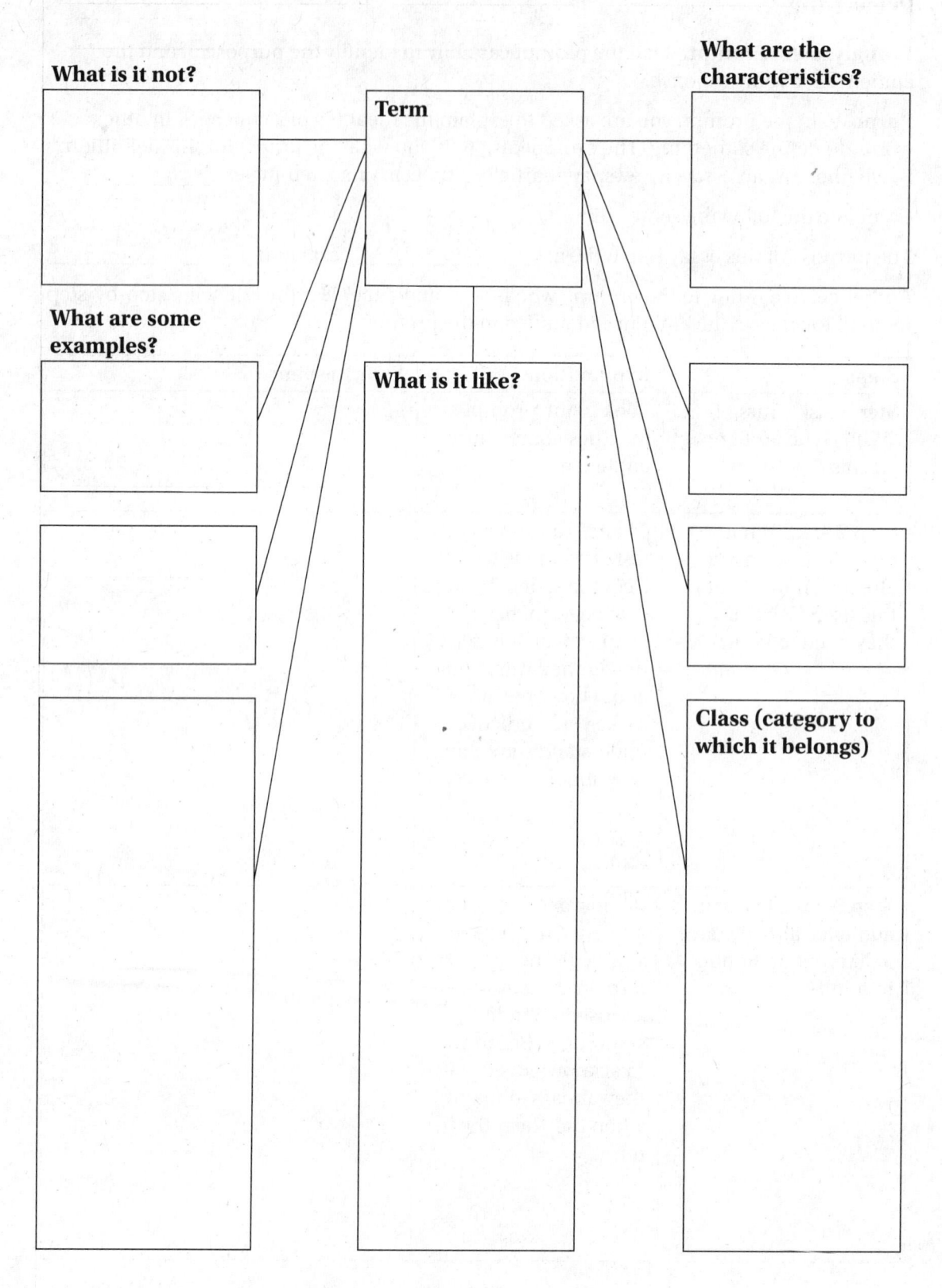

What is it not?

Term

What are the characteristics?

What are some examples?

What is it like?

Class (category to which it belongs)

3. Develop a Thesis. Your response will involve defining a common concept in an uncommon way. Your thesis statement will reflect the distinction between the common definition and your extended definition. Read the following sample thesis:

> The dictionary defines *courage* as a state of mind that enables one to face danger without fear. **However,** I think that that courage has more to do with the ability to face danger *in spite* of fear.

Use words like *but, however,* or *although* to draw the distinction between the common definition and your extended definition. Write your thesis on the lines below.

_____
_____
_____
_____

NOTE: You do not have to start with the dictionary's definition of the term. You can, for example, start with what people commonly think, or what you saw on TV or read in the paper, and take off from that point.

4. Organize Your Ideas. By now you have lots of information for your response: examples, anecdotes, quotations, and so on. The organizational plan you choose will depend on your thesis. Here are some possibilities:

From dictionary definition to personal definition—when you want to show that your definition is richer or more accurate than the one in the dictionary

From negative definition to positive definition—when you want to surprise your audience or cast a positive light on a term commonly thought of as negative.

From positive definition to negative definition—see above.

From personal anecdote to what other say, or vice versa—when you want to compare or contrast opinions

Chronological order—when you want to discuss how the meaning of a term has changed over time

Order of importance—when you want to present various aspects of a concept, either from the least important (or convincing) to the most important (or convincing), or vice versa

Drafting Your Response

Use the following framework to draft your response to the writing prompt. Write your draft on the lined page that follows.

Framework	Directions and Explanations
Introduction	
• Use an attention grabber. • Supply necessary background information, including your subject's larger category. • Provide a clear thesis.	**Get your readers' attention** Use an arresting example or a striking contrast. **Build background** Provide background information and mention the common dictionary definition of the term. **Get to the point** State your thesis, showing how your definition extends the common one and indicating how your essay will progress.
Body	
• Discuss the first example, illustration, anecdote, or analogy. • Discuss the second example, and so on.	**Offer some support** Provide examples that bolster your thesis. **Organize your ideas** Arrange those examples in an order that makes sense, such as chronological order or order of importance.
Conclusion	
• Summarize the definition. • Briefly explain the extended definition.	**Sum it up** Quickly remind your readers of your extended definition, and highlight the ways in which your definition is different from the common definition. **Provide your opinion** Leave readers with a clear statement of your ideas about what the term really means.

Draft your response in the space below.

Evaluating, Revising, and Editing Your Response

Use the following strategies to evaluate and revise your response. You may make your revisions directly on your first draft, or, if necessary, write your revised draft on the lined pages that follow.

Evaluation Guidelines for Extended-Definition Response		
Evaluation Question	**Tips**	**Revision Techniques**
1. Does this response have a clear thesis?	Underline the thesis statement in the essay.	If necessary, **add** a thesis statement to the essay.
2. Is the response organized appropriately, to reflect the purpose?	Look back at the type of organization pattern you selected in prewriting.	**Rearrange** information to fit the type of organization pattern you selected in the prewriting phase.
3. Does the response use specific details to support the thesis?	Place a dot next to each example, illustration, and so on.	**Elaborate** on the thesis by adding details.
4. Does the response contain only information that clearly supports the topic?	Lightly circle each dot that shows the thesis is true.	**Cut** elaborations that do not relate to your thesis.
5. Are ideas logically related to one another? Are there gaps in logic or information?	Study the flow from one sentence to the next. Does each idea follow logically from the one before it?	**Add** details to fill in gaps in logic. **Add** transitions to improve the flow of ideas.
6. Does the response use appropriate, precise vocabulary?	Identify words that represent a stretch for you. If you are not certain of the word's meaning, revise.	**Replace** words that you are uncertain about with words that are more familiar.
7. Does the response use a variety of sentence structures?	Identify at least 1 compound sentence (2 main clauses) and 1 complex (1 independent + 1 dependent clause) per paragraph	**Combine** ideas to create compound or complex sentences.

Draft your revised response in the space below.

Proofing Your Response

Final Editing Guidelines

Proofread your response to ensure that it

- contains only complete sentences, no fragments.
- shows proper subject-verb agreement, consistent verb tense, and correct use of nominative and subjective case.
- uses correct capitalization, punctuation, and spelling.

Draft your final response in the space below.

WRITING PROMPT 4

Plan, write, and proofread a descriptive essay in response to the writing prompt below.

A local amusement park is holding a contest. The winner will receive a free season pass to the amusement park. Read the instructions for the contest and then write an essay to enter it.

> What is your favorite ride or activity at the amusement park? Write an essay telling all about it. Use descriptive words and appeal to all our senses. Make the reader want to try out the ride or activity.

As you write your essay, remember to

- Identify the ride or activity.
- Use sensory imagery—appeal to the reader's sense of sight, smell, hearing, touch, and taste.
- Consider the audience and purpose for your response.
- Organize your response so that your ideas progress logically.
- Proofread your response to correct errors in grammar, spelling, and punctuation.

STRATEGY FOR RESPONDING TO THE PROMPT

Prewriting

1. Analyze the Prompt. Read the prompt carefully to identify the purpose of and the audience for your response.

Purpose. In the prompt, you are asked to write a descriptive essay for a contest. The prompt also tells what your essay should be about.

Complete the following sentence:

The purpose of this essay is to write a _____ describing _____ .

Audience. This prompt offers clues about the audience. Use the following step-by-step method to analyze the audience identified in the prompt.

Steps	Explanation	Your Response
Step 1 Ask yourself, "Who is the audience for this essay?"	Look to the prompt for clues about your audience.	
Step 2 Ask, "What does my audience already know about the topic? What do they want me to tell them?"	Since the reader works for the amusement park, he or she is likely to know a lot about the ride or activity. Your challenge will be to describe it in a way that is interesting and creative. Also, the reader wants to know what you find exciting, so be sure to give details that show why you like the ride or activity.	
Step 3 Ask, "What is the appropriate format or style of writing for this audience?"	Think about the audience. Should you use formal or informal language?	

2. Brainstorm Details You will need to list different details about the ride or activity. Write the name of the ride or activity in the center circle of the graphic organizer. Then write different details in the outer circles. Think about how you feel, what you see, and what you hear.

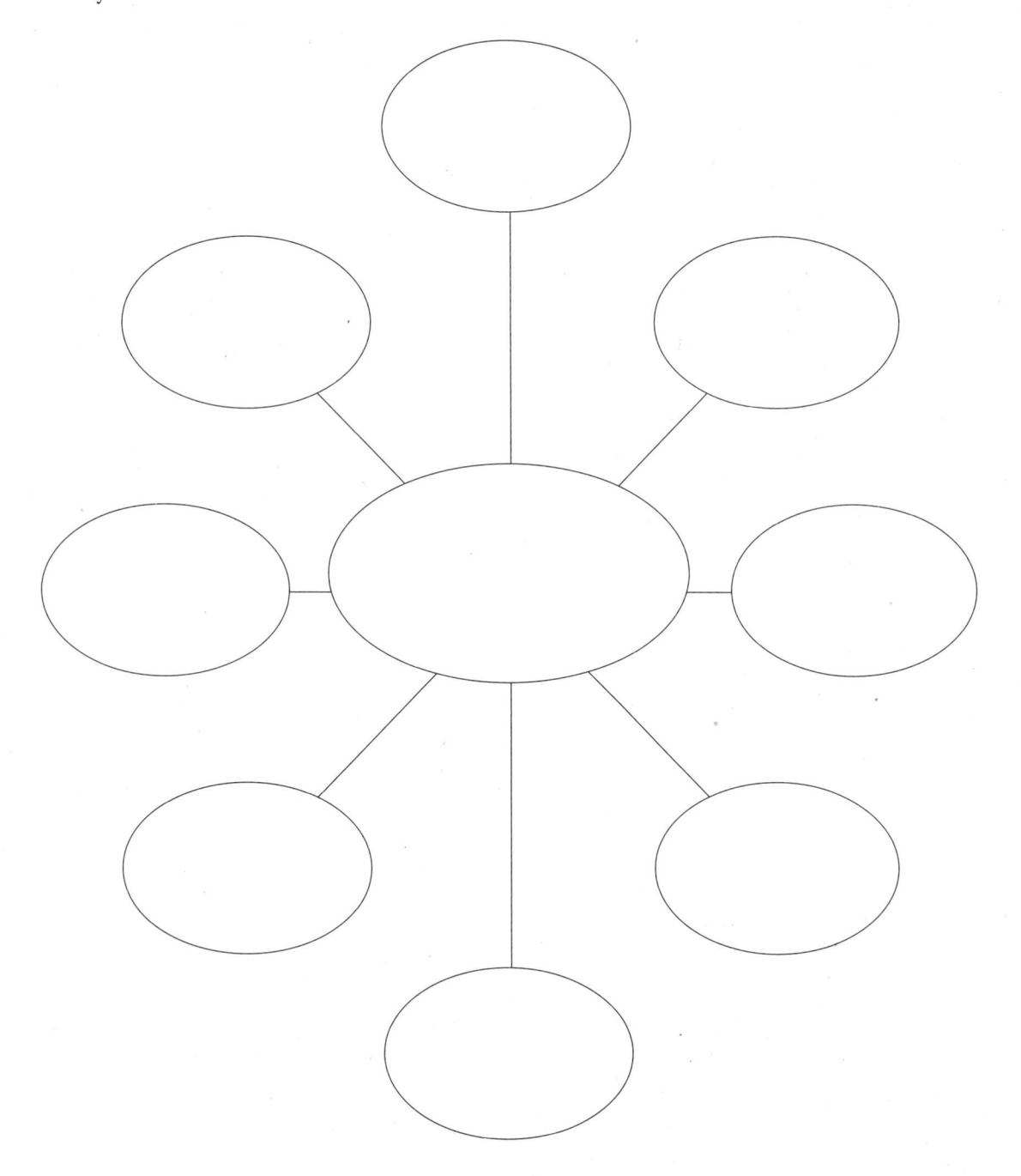

3. Develop a Thesis While a descriptive essay does not necessarily always have a thesis, this writing prompt asks a question that requires one. You will need to formulate a thesis statement about why this ride or activity is your favorite. Write your thesis statement on the line below.

_____

4. Organize Your Response. You have details for your descriptive essay as well as a thesis statement. Now you need to decide how to organize your response. Here are some possibilities:

From general to specific— when you want to present more popular, or general ideas, about the ride or activity and then present your own specific ideas.

Chronological order— when you want to describe the ride or activity in time order, from the time you get on line (or buy a ticket) until you finish the ride or activity.

Spatial order— when you want to describe something as you observe it, from left to right or top to bottom.

Order of importance— when you want to describe something from the least important detail to the most important detail, or vice versa.

Use the chart below to organize your descriptive details. Decide how you will organize your essay. Then list each detail in the chart. Use the right column to order your details.

How I will organize my essay: _____

Detail	Order

Drafting Your Response

Use the following framework to draft your response to the writing prompt. Write your draft on the lined page that follows.

Framework	Directions and Explanations
Introduction	
• Identify the topic.	**Name the ride or activity** Tell the reader what this essay will describe. Include your thesis statement about what makes the ride or activity so special.
Body	
• Describe the first aspect of the ride or activity, and so on.	**Organize your descriptions** Arrange your details in an order that makes sense. Begin by describing the first detail completely. Then move on to the next detail.
• Use sensory images.	**Appeal to the senses** Be sure to include descriptions that appeal to the different senses.
Conclusion	
• Restate your thesis.	**Sum it up** Briefly remind the reader why you like this ride so much.

Draft your response in the space below.

Evaluating, Revising, and Editing Your Response

Use the following strategies to evaluate and revise your response. You may make your revisions directly on your first draft, or if necessary, write your revised draft on the lined pages that follow.

Evaluation Guidelines for Essay Response		
Evaluation Question	**Tips**	**Revision Techniques**
1. Is the response written in the correct format to address the prompt?	Ask yourself, "Is my response a real descriptive essay?"	If necessary, add descriptive details about the ride or activity.
2. Is the response organized appropriately, to reflect the purpose?	Look back at the type of organization pattern you selected in prewriting.	**Rearrange** information to fit the type of organization pattern you selected in the prewriting phase.
3. Does the response have a clear thesis?	Ask yourself, "Does my response clearly tell which ride or activity I like most and why?"	If necessary, **add** a thesis statement to your essay. Or **rewrite** your thesis statement so that it clearly answers the question in the prompt.
4. Are ideas logically related to one another? Are there gaps in logic or information?	Study the flow from one sentence to the next. Does each idea follow logically from the one before it?	**Add** details to fill in gaps in logic. Use **transition words** or phrases to improve the flow of ideas.
5. Does the response appeal to all five senses?	Read your narrative to look for descriptions that appeal to each of the senses. You may find it helpful to list the senses and put a check mark for each description that appeals to it.	**Add** descriptions if needed.
6. Does the response use appropriate, precise vocabulary?	Identify words that are tired or overused by circling them.	**Replace** the circled words with more descriptive ones.
7. Does the response use a variety of sentence structures?	Look for sentences that start with different types of phrases. Underline sentences that seem to repeat the same structure.	**Rewrite** some of the sentences so that some of them begin with dependent clauses.

Draft your revised response in the space below.

Proofing Your Response

Final Editing Guidelines

Proofread your response to ensure that it

- contains only complete sentences, no fragments.
- shows proper subject-verb agreement, consistent verb tense, and correct use of nominative and subjective case.
- uses correct capitalization, punctuation, and spelling.

Draft your final response in the space below.

WRITING CONVENTIONS PRACTICE 1

Identify the type of error, if any, in each underlined passage. Use the provided answer sheet at the end of the workbook to record your answers, and use a separate sheet of paper to record your response to the open-ended question.

The Journal of Friar Junipero Serra

<u>In 1769 the Franciscan missionary Friar</u>[1] Junipero <u>Serra accompanyed Gaspar de Portola to what became</u>[2] <u>San Diego California.</u>[3] In the journal Serra kept, he noted the many difficulties <u>travelers in that region faced. Serra</u>[4] realized that the land and climate were comfortable for living and raising crops. He also said <u>there was "good and abundant water, sufficient for a town.</u>[5] Since the explorers hoped to <u>found a Mission, this is important.</u>[6]

Writing Conventions Practice 1

1. A Spelling
   B Capitalization
   C Punctuation
   D No error

2. A Spelling
   B Capitalization
   C Punctuation
   D No error

3. A Spelling
   B Capitalization
   C Punctuation
   D No error

4. A Spelling
   B Capitalization
   C Punctuation
   D No error

5. A Spelling
   B Capitalization
   C Punctuation
   D No error

6. Rewrite the last sentence correctly.

WRITING CONVENTIONS PRACTICE 2

Identify the correct words to fill in the blanks in each underlined passage. Use the provided answer sheet at the end of the workbook to record your answers, and use a separate sheet of paper to record your response to the open-ended question.

> Women in the 1800s __(1)__ vote nor sit on juries. Married women in many states __(2)__ little or no control over their own property and most __(3)__ did not attend school. Grimké __(4)__ "In most families, it is considered a matter of far more consequence to call a girl off from making a pie, or a pudding, than to interrupt __(5)__ whilst engaged in her studies. Grimké, just like feminists today, __(6)__ women would achieve much more than perfect pies.

Writing Conventions Practice 2

1. A had no
   B could not
   C do not
   D will not

2. A had
   B has
   C have
   D haves

3. A woman
   B womans
   C women
   D women's

4. A wrote;
   B wrote.
   C wrote'
   D wrote

5. A it
   B them
   C she
   D her

6. Using the correct form of the verb *to know,* rewrite the fourth sentence (sentence with blank 6).

WRITING CONVENTIONS PRACTICE 3

Identify the type of error, if any, in each underlined passage. Use the provided answer sheet at the end of the workbook to record your answers, and use a separate sheet of paper to record your response to the open-ended question.

A Shawnee Leader Seeks Allies

When the <u>grate Shawnee leader Tecumseh</u> spoke <u>to the Osage</u>
                1   2

<u>people</u> <u>he had a plan,</u> for unity among the tribes. <u>Tecummseh</u>
  3   4

<u>came from a</u> Shawnee family who lost its men fighting the settlers.

Tecumseh saw that the Indians' days <u>were numbered they would</u>
                              5

not survive if they did not stand together. The speech he made to

the Osage shows <u>how carefull Tecumseh</u> considered the situation of
                  6

his people.

Writing Conventions Practice 3

1. A Spelling
   B Capitalization
   C Punctuation
   D No error

2. A Spelling
   B Capitalization
   C Punctuation
   D No error

3. A Spelling
   B Capitalization
   C Punctuation
   D No error

4. A Spelling
   B Capitalization
   C Punctuation
   D No error

5. A Spelling
   B Capitalization
   C Punctuation
   D No error

6. Rewrite the fourth sentence correctly (includes underlined passage 6).

WRITING CONVENTIONS PRACTICE 4

Identify the correct words to fill in the blanks in each underlined passage. Use the provided answer sheet at the end of the workbook to record your answers, and use a separate sheet of paper to record your response to the open-ended question.

Declaring Independence

A fascinating women of the __(1)__ was Abigail Adams. This young lady from Massachusetts __(2)__ some of the most __(3)__ letters about this important time in American __(4)__ was a __(5)__. In many ways, Abigail Adams __(6)__ what made a people independent.

Writing Conventions Practice 4

1. A revolutionary period
   B Revolutionary period
   C revolutionary Period
   D Revolutionary Period

2. A pens
   B had penned
   C pen
   D penned

3. A memrable
   B memorable
   C memoryable
   D memorible

4. A history it
   B history; it
   C history, it
   D history. It

5. A time of struggle and change
   B times struggling and changing
   C timing for struggle and change
   D time of struggle, and change

6. Using the correct form of the verb *to show*, rewrite the last sentence (sentence with blank 6).

WRITING CONVENTIONS PRACTICE 5

Read each question and choose the ***best*** answer. Use the provided answer sheet at the end of the workbook to record your answers.

1. Choose the sentence that shows the capital letters used correctly.

    A It's sort of confusing, because Pisa's nickname is peesh and her dog's name is Peenie.

    B It's sort of confusing, because Pisa's nickname is Peesh and her dog's name is Peenie.

    C It's sort of confusing, because Pisa's nickname is Peesh and her dog's name is peenie.

    D It's sort of confusing, because Pisa's Nickname is Peesh and her dog's name is Peenie.

2. Choose the word or words that ***best*** complete the sentence.

    Tessa, one of the Norris twins, _____ to eat corn on the cob.

    A lovely

    B loving

    C love

    D loves

3. Find the sentence that is complete and is written correctly.

    A Drink a warm drink, you will warm up.

    B If you snuggle under the blanket.

    C If you snuggle under a blanket and drink a warm drink, you will warm up.

    D If you snuggle under a blanket and drink a warm drink, warm up.

4. Choose the answer that shows the correct punctuation.

   A Yao said "Let's leave for the wedding at 10:00".

   B Yao said, "Let's leave for the wedding at 10:00."

   C Yao said "Let's leave for the wedding at 10:00."

   D Yao said, "Lets leave for the wedding at 10:00."

5. Choose the answer that shows the correct capitalization.

   A Hannah lives in the East. Her home is just south of New York City.

   B Hannah lives in the east. Her home is just south of New York City.

   C Hannah lives in the east. Her home is just South of New York City.

   D Hannah lives in the East. Her home is just south of New York city.

6. Which sentence is complete and is written correctly?

   A Everyone with tickets to the seven o' clock movie, should move to the front of the line.

   B Everyone, with tickets to the seven o' clock movie should move to the front of the line.

   C Everyone with tickets to the seven o' clock movie should move to the front of the line.

   D Everyone with tickets, to the seven o' clock movie should move to the front of the line.

7. Read this sentence. If you were editing, what would be the **most** important thing to change?

   We were all so board that we actually went out and played in the sandbox like small children.

   A   Place a comma before <u>and</u>.

   B   Replace <u>were</u> with <u>was</u>.

   C   Separate <u>sandbox</u> into two words.

   D   Replace <u>board</u> with <u>bored</u>.

8. Read this sentence. Based on the antecedent, identify the pronoun that belongs in the blank.

   If you ask a teacher, _____ will tell you that grades will matter some day.

   A   he or she

   B   they

   C   who

   D   them

9. Read this paragraph. Choose the sentence that does not belong in the paragraph.

   (1) Could you sleep standing up if you had a good grip on a tree limb? (2) If not, you would not make a very good owl! (3) Of course, human beings can't really be owls anyhow. (4) If you ever happen upon an owl roosting on a tree limb during the daytime, take note of its claws. (5) They will be tightly gripped around the tree limb so the owl does not fall. (6) Even in its sleeping state, an owl can maintain this safety grip.

   A   Sentence 2

   B   Sentence 3

   C   Sentence 4

   D   Sentence 5

10. Choose the word that shows improper grammar.

    Jace <u>joined</u> Mitchell and <u>I</u> for the 2:00 <u>movie</u> at the dollar <u>theater</u> near my house.
          A   B   C   D

    A   joined

    B   I

    C   movie

    D   theater

11. Choose the *best* way to combine these two sentences.

    She wore red mittens with her navy blue coat.
    She wore a red scarf with her navy blue coat.

    A   She wore red mittens with her navy blue coat and red scarf.

    B   She wore red mittens with her navy blue coat and also a red scarf.

    C   She wore a navy blue coat and red mittens and a red scarf.

    D   She wore a red scarf and red mittens with her navy blue coat.

12. Choose the sentence that is written correctly.

    A   The tee shirt slogen said, "Cavman, Martian, or Super Hero? Yes!"

    B   The tee shirt slogan said, "Caveman, Marshen, or Super Hero? Yes!"

    C   The tee shirt slogan said, "Caveman, Martian, or Super Hero? Yes!"

    D   The tee shirt slogan said, "Caveman, Martian, or Super Heero? Yes!"

13. Choose the sentence that *best* fills the blank in the paragraph.

    Jon was looking for a new pair of binoculars. _____. The high bid was $16.00. He put in a bid of $17.00 and then he watched. At 8 minutes left, nothing had happened. It was the same at 6 minutes, 4 minutes, and 2 minutes. Then, at 1 minute and 30 seconds, someone bid $18.00. Jon watched. At 1 minute, someone bid $19.00. Jon watched. At 30 seconds, someone bid $20.00. Jon watched. At 10 seconds left, Jon entered $21.00, and then he watched again. He counted 9-8-7-6-5-4-3-.... His auction window flicked.... had someone beat his bid? No! On the screen, he saw, "You are the winning bidder." Jon cheered!

    A   He looked at the department store near his house.

    B   He had dropped his old pair of binoculars, and they weren't working very well.

    C   He asked his friends if they knew of a good deal on binoculars.

    D   He went online and discovered a pair was being sold at auction and had 10 minutes left.

14. For what reason might a person write a short fiction story?

    A   to entertain

    B   to inform

    C   to persuade

    D   to apologize

15. In which of these written pieces would it make the *most* sense to use second person throughout?

    A   a front-page newspaper article

    B   a mystery novel

    C   a paper for an English class

    D   a recipe book

Indiana Grade 9 Practice test

Reading And Writing

Read the selection below. Then read each question and choose the best answer. Use a separate sheet of paper to record your response to the open ended question.

Christina's New Job

When she put down the phone, Christina's hands were shaking. She couldn't believe her luck. She would actually be spending the summer working as a member of a white-water rafting crew in the Grand Canyon! Twenty minutes ago she had been contemplating another boring job as a waitress at one of the dreary local restaurants, but now she began to imagine the glamorous adventures she would have in the next three months.

The remaining weeks of the school year passed in a blur of excitement. Before she could believe it, Christina was standing on the banks of the mighty Colorado River. She spent four days training for her new job with John and Marty, the husband-and-wife team that would constitute her small family for the summer. She had patiently sorted gear, planned menus, shopped for supplies, and waterproofed the special bags that would hold the supplies. She had been an attentive student, but she secretly wondered whether all her responsibilities would be so mundane. When she had taken the job, she had had more exciting challenges in mind.

As she gazed down the river into the famous canyon, she thought about all the brave explorers who had journeyed through it. Her mind filled with images of their heroic exploits, and she thought, with a little shiver of pleasure, of the fabulous stories she would have to tell all her jealous friends back home. Surely, her job would become more interesting.

However, the first morning of the journey down the river was calm and uneventful. Of course, the scenery was spectacular, and the fifteen passengers were nice people. There was no one Christina's age in the group, though. Surrounded by the magnificence of the canyon and the powerful river, she felt a twinge of loneliness. Had she made a mistake about the glamour of this summer job?

Suddenly, as the raft approached the first of many white-water rapids, it made a twisting turn in the current. "Look out!" Marty yelled. "Everybody hang on!" She desperately tried to swerve the raft away from a boulder in the middle of the river, but the stern struck the rock. The motor made a loud grinding noise.

"Propeller's smashed!" yelled John over the roar of the rapids. "We'll have to let the current push us over to the riverbank. We've got a spare motor, but it'll take some time to put it on." The passengers clutched the sides of the raft and stared, wide-eyed and silent, at John and Marty as the raft drifted to the sheer cliff that edged the river. "Come on, Christina," John called when they reached the shore, "climb out onto the cliff and hang onto this rope. Loop it around that overhanging rock and hold on tight. Marty and I will change the motor while you keep us anchored."

Christina gulped as she jumped from the raft. Her heart was racing as she looped the rope and braced herself against a rock. Things were certainly getting more interesting.

Marty and John quickly removed the smashed motor and swung the replacement into place. Then, just as Christina breathed a sigh of relief, another twist of the current struck the raft broadside and jerked the rope from her hands. She stared in disbelief as the raft swiftly flowed downstream, leaving her stranded on the narrow cliff edge. She felt seventeen pairs of eyes staring at her. Marty yelled something to her, but Christina couldn't distinguish the words over the roar of the rapids.

The twenty minutes that it took to connect the spare motor and maneuver the raft up the river to recover her were the longest minutes of Christina's life. The shock of finding herself trapped on a tiny ledge above the furious rapids was balanced only by the embarrassment she felt for losing her hold on the rope. Marty gave Christina a hug as Christina jumped onto the raft, and John smiled. "I'm sure glad it happened to you instead of me," he said.

That evening as Christina helped the passengers set up their tents on a sandy beach, she was in a reflective mood. Even though her knees still felt a little rubbery, she felt good about the work she had done throughout the afternoon, and she had acquired a new respect for the power of nature. By the time John had finished grilling steaks for dinner and everyone was relaxing, Christina had made a rule for herself: Focus on doing the job instead of on romantic daydreams.

Christina's New Job

1. John and Marty handle the loss of their propeller
   - ○ angrily.
   - ○ joyfully.
   - ○ calmly.
   - ○ frantically.

2. Which sentence did the author use to show that losing one's grip on the rope was not viewed as an incompetent act?
   - ○ Marty yelled something to her, but Christina couldn't distinguish the words.
   - ○ She felt seventeen pairs of eyes staring at her.
   - ○ "I'm sure glad it happened to you instead of me," he said.
   - ○ She stared in disbelief as the raft swiftly flowed downstream.

3. In the second half of the story, the author uses words like *desperately*, *grinding*, *jerked*, and *clutched*. How do such words contribute to the mood of the story?
   - ○ The words emphasize the turbulent setting that is developing.
   - ○ The words emphasize Christina's mistake.
   - ○ The words make it sound as if Christina is trying too hard to find excitement.
   - ○ The words make it sound as if working at a restaurant would have been more fun.

Christina's New Job

4 In the second paragraph, how does the word *patiently* describe Christina's feelings about her first task at her new job?

　○ She almost lost her temper.

　○ The work was so hard that she struggled.

　○ She had to check herself to do the task without feeling bored.

　○ She had to slow herself down so she wouldn't look rushed.

5 Based on the context of the first paragraph, the word *contemplating* means

　○ hoping to find.

　○ thinking about.

　○ looking forward to.

　○ singing the praises of.

6 Why were Christina's hands shaking when she hung up the phone at the beginning of the story?

　○ She is happy to have been invited to go on a summer vacation.

　○ She is excited about the offer of an interesting summer job.

　○ She is upset that she has to spend the summer working at a local restaurant.

　○ She seldom receives any calls at all so she doesn't know how to handle it.

7 What is MOST ironic about the ending of the selection?

Read the selection below. Then read each question and choose the best answer. Use a separate sheet of paper to record your responses to the open-ended question.

A Narrow Fellow in the Grass
Emily Dickinson

A narrow fellow in the grass
Occasionally rides;
You may have met him—did you not?
His notice sudden is.

5   The grass divides as with a comb,
A spotted shaft is seen;
And then it closes at your feet
And opens further on.

He likes a boggy acre,
10   A floor too cool for corn.
Yet when a boy, and barefoot,
I more than once, at noon,

Have passed, I thought, a whip-lash
Unbraiding in the sun—
15   When, stooping to secure it,
It wrinkled, and was gone.

Several of nature's people
I know, and they know me;
I feel for them a transport[1]
20   Of cordiality;

But never met this fellow,
Attended or alone,
Without a tighter breathing,
And zero at the bone.

---

1. transport: feeling of deep pleasure

A Narrow Fellow in the Grass

8 The point of view in this poem is

○ second person.

○ first person.

○ third person limited.

○ third person omniscient.

9 What does *"zero at the bone"* mean?

○ fear

○ cold

○ apathy

○ sympathy

10 The *"narrow fellow in the grass"* is a

○ worm.

○ toad.

○ snake.

○ mouse.

11 The poem's speaker is

○ Dickinson the adult poet.

○ Dickinson as a child.

○ A grown man.

○ A young boy.

A Narrow Fellow in the Grass

12 How would this poem MOST LIKELY differ if it were an ode?

○ It would be much longer.

○ It would describe all the great qualities of the narrow fellow.

○ Every pair of lines would rhyme.

○ The narrow fellow would symbolize a dead hero.

13 What does the poet mean by *nature's people* in line 17?

○ animals

○ plants

○ friends and neighbors

○ moon and stars

14 How does this poem reflect Emily Dickinson's secluded lifestyle?

Canada's History and Culture

As in the United States, Native American societies were once found across Canada. The first Europeans to sail to Canada's eastern shores were Viking adventurers. They visited between A.D. 1000 and as late as the mid-1300s. However, the Vikings left no permanent settlements. More extensive exploration by Europeans began in 1497. In that year John Cabot explored the coasts of Newfoundland and other islands for the English.

The first great European explorer of Canada's interior was Jacques Cartier (zhahk kahr-TYAY) of France. In the 1530s he traveled up the St. Lawrence River as far as present-day Montreal. This was nearly a century before the English established colonies in New England. The French had three main goals in Canada. First, they wanted to find a northwest water passage across North America to Asia. Second, they wanted to exploit nearby fishing waters and to develop a trade for animal furs from North America. Third, they wanted to convert Canadian Indians to Roman Catholicism.

By 1608 the French established a permanent settlement at what became Quebec City on the St. Lawrence River. Soon, French settlers were farming along the St. Lawrence and in nearby Nova Scotia to the east.

In 1713 Great Britain took over Nova Scotia. Eventually, the British forced many French settlers there to leave. After a long war, Britain had won control of all of French Canada by 1763. The British organized Canada into several governmental districts called provinces. Today Canada has 10 provinces and three special territories.

British settlement in Canada increased during the American Revolution. Many colonists left the United States so they could stay under British rule. Canada's population continued to grow in the first half of the 1800s. Immigration from abroad increased. In 1867 the British government created the self-governing Dominion of Canada. The dominion included the provinces of Ontario, Quebec, Nova Scotia, and New Brunswick. Manitoba, British Columbia, and Prince Edward Island joined them in the 1870s. Alberta and Saskatchewan did not become provinces until 1905. Newfoundland became part of Canada in 1949.

Canada's History and Culture

15 Which statement supports the idea that England was NOT power hungry?

○ In 1867 the British government created the self-governing Dominion of Canada.

○ Eventually, the British forced many French settlers there to leave.

○ British settlement in Canada increased during the American Revolution.

○ This was nearly a century before the English established colonies in New England.

16 Based on the context of the first paragraph, *extensive* means

○ long-lasting.

○ purposeful.

○ far-ranging.

○ scientific.

17 What is the BEST summary of the passage's second paragraph?

○ France sent Jacques Cartier to explore Canada's interior to prepare for a French presence that could develop a trade in animal furs and convert Canadian Indians to Roman Catholicism.

○ Jacques Cartier, who looked for a passage across North America to Asia nearly a century before the English established colonies in New England, was a great explorer.

○ The French, motivated by their desire to convert Canadian Indians to Roman Catholicism, sent Jacques Cartier to travel up the St. Lawrence River as far as present-day Montreal.

○ France sent Jacques Cartier to explore Canada's interior to find a passage across North America to Asia and to prepare for a French presence that could develop a trade in animal furs and convert Canadian Indians to Roman Catholicism.

Canada's History and Culture

18 Which of these questions could MOST LIKELY be answered by doing further research on the main topic of this passage?

○ What are some major differences between Viking and U.S. cultures?

○ How did the colonists' migration to Canada impact the country?

○ Should Canadians who trace their lineage back to the American colonies before the American Revolution be granted U.S. citizenship?

○ Why didn't the Vikings come to what is now the U.S.?

19 Which event would go in the blank space on this time line?

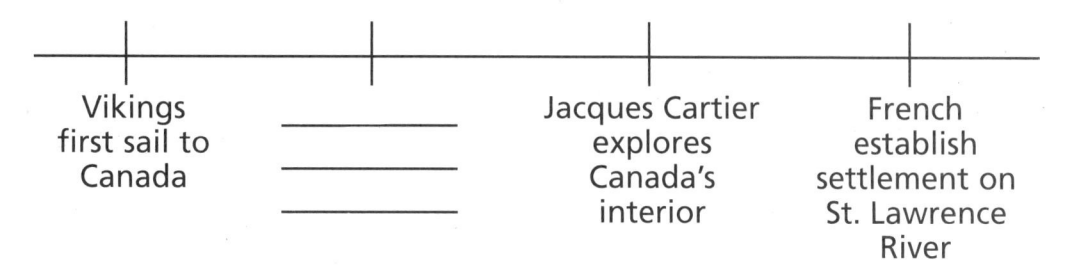

| Vikings first sail to Canada | _____ | Jacques Cartier explores Canada's interior | French establish settlement on St. Lawrence River |

○ Britain wins control over all of French Canada

○ John Cabot explores Newfoundland

○ Alberta becomes a Canadian province

○ Great Britain takes over Nova Scotia

20 Based on the title, which of these topics would you LEAST expect to find in the passage?

○ geography of Canada

○ Canadian foods

○ Canadian customs

○ Canadian wars

Canada's History and Culture

21 Based on the passage, why did some colonists move from what would be the United States to Canada during the American Revolution?

Read the selection below. Then read each question and choose the best answer. Use a separate sheet of paper to record your responses to the open-ended question.

Seeing Stars Over Light Pollution
An Editorial

Marc lives in a sunny city in the southwestern United States. After sunset, though, his parents will not let him ride his bike, jog to a friend's house three streets away, or even walk his dog. Marc's parents say the neighborhood is too dark. One evening a neighbor was robbed walking home from a bus stop. She could not describe the mugger, even though street lights line every block of her route. Unfortunately, the lights are fitted with sodium-vapor lamps, and she could barely see in their dim, pinkish glow.

(2) Marc's neighbor became a victim of the near-useless lamps that her city installed. The city is required by law to combat light pollution with dimmer street lights. Actions taken by city and state legislators to prevent light pollution are well meant, but so far they cause bigger problems than they solve. Until better solutions are found, prevention of light pollution should not be required by law.

(3) It is true that light pollution is a serious problem. Astronomers have discussed it with the United Nations. They point out that even the most advanced telescopes work poorly when city lights keep the night sky bright. Nighttime satellite photos show the United States clearly outlined in light. Cities, suburbs, and highways cast their combined glow into space. All this brightness, scientists warn, overwhelms the fainter light signals reaching Earth from the rest of the universe. The light is also a wasteful use of precious fossil fuels.

In the Middle East, religious leaders find that city lights make it hard to see the pale sliver of new moon that signals the start of the Muslim holy month. In the Arctic, researchers discover that native people are less likely to teach star-related cultural traditions to the young because street lights now blot out important stars. Since star lore is central to their culture, their traditional system of passing knowledge from generation to generation is at risk.

Clearly, light pollution is a problem, but state and local governments in the United States have taken action too hastily without weighing the consequences. What happened in Marc's neighborhood is an unfortunate result of this haste. Many cities across the nation have new "glare control" laws. The entire states of Maine, New Mexico, and Arizona have laws against glare. These laws limit the kinds of outdoor lighting that people can use in public areas, businesses, and even private yards.

One reason that glare control should not be required by law is expense. It is often taxpayers who foot the bills for these measures. Some laws require expensive glare shields for the tops of all outdoor lights. Glare shields aim the light rays straight downward rather than outward to brighten a wider area. Other laws demand certain types of expensive lighting, such as the sodium-vapor lights in Marc's neighborhood. Still other laws forbid certain types of less-expensive lighting, such as mercury-vapor lights. This type of lighting is low in cost because it requires fewer repairs than sodium-vapor lights, but it is considered high in glare.

Safety is another important reason why glare-control laws are a problem. Glare is linked to brightness. Cut down on glare, and you get dimmer lights that lead to bigger safety problems. Drivers have a harder time avoiding hazards on poorly lit roads. Common sense tells us that crime increases on darkened sidewalks. In their rush to take action, many government leaders have failed to give these drawbacks careful consideration. They have neglected to search for better solutions. Instead, they seem to think that glare control is more important than safety.

(8) Without question, the need to control light pollution is real. The world's scientists should be able to observe the universe, and native peoples should be able to maintain their cultural traditions. At the same time, the need for safe streets and safe neighborhoods is also real. People should be able to walk safely down well-lit streets at night. Surely the same technology that gives us advanced telescopes can also give us safe, inexpensive lighting for our homes, parks, streets, cities, and highways—and still let us gaze at the stars.

Seeing Stars Over Light Pollution An Editorial

22 What BEST shows that this passage is an editorial?

○ It describes light pollution.

○ It gives an anecdote about a person who was robbed.

○ It describes cultural traditions.

○ It gives an opinion about a problem and the laws that are used to solve it.

23 Why does the author begin the selection telling about Marc not being able to go out at night and about the neighbor being mugged?

○ to appeal to readers' emotions

○ to scare readers into staying in at night

○ to show how paranoid Marc's parents are

○ to make the story exciting

24 The speaker's mood throughout the selection is

○ light and fun.

○ serious, but light.

○ angry, but reasonable.

○ accusatory and livids

25 Take a close look at the title and first line of the selection. What types of words did the author choose?

○ words with homophones

○ words with alliteration

○ words that rhyme

○ words with similar meanings

Copyright © by Holt, Rinehart and Winston. All rights reserved.

Seeing Stars Over Light Pollution An Editorial

26 Which of these questions does the writer want the reader to ask about controlling light pollution?

○ Why doesn't the government do more to solve this problem?

○ Why is everyone worried about light pollution, anyway?

○ Do we really need bright lights at night?

○ How can we make sure our solutions really help people?

27 What is the purpose of this selection?

○ to persuade people that street lights need to be brighter

○ to persuade people that teenagers have to be allowed to be out at night

○ to complain about glare-control laws

○ to ask for funding for new streetlights

Read the selection below. Then read each question and choose the best answer. Use a separate sheet of paper to record your responses to the open-ended and critical thinking questions.

from The Open Window
by Saki

"My aunt will be down presently, Mr. Nuttel," said a very self-possessed young lady of fifteen; "in the meantime you must try and put up with me.

Framton Nuttel endeavored to say the correct something which should duly flatter the niece of the moment without unduly discounting the aunt that was to come. Privately he doubted more than ever whether these formal visits on a succession of total strangers would do much toward helping the nerve cure which he was supposed to be undergoing.

"I know how it will be," his sister had said when he was preparing to migrate to this rural retreat; "you will bury yourself down there and not speak to a living soul, and your nerves will be worse than ever from moping. I shall just give you letters of introduction to all the people I know there. Some of them, as far as I can remember, were quite nice."

Framton wondered whether Mrs. Sappleton, the lady to whom he was presenting one of the letters of introduction, came into the nice division.

"Do you know many of the people round here?" asked the niece, when she judged that they had had sufficient silent communion.

"Hardly a soul," said Framton. "My sister was staying here, at the rectory, you know, some four years ago, and she gave me letters of introduction to some of the people here."

He made the last statement in a tone of distinct regret.

"Then you know practically nothing about my aunt?" pursued the self-possessed young lady.

"Only her name and address," admitted the caller. He was wondering whether Mrs. Sappleton was in the married or widowed state. An undefinable something about the room seemed to suggest masculine habitation.

"Her great tragedy happened just three years ago," said the child; "that would be since your sister's time."

"Her tragedy?" asked Framton; somehow, in this restful country spot, tragedies seemed out of place.

"You may wonder why we keep that window wide open on an October afternoon," said the niece, indicating a large French window that opened onto a lawn.

"It is quite warm for the time of the year," said Framton, "but has that window got anything to do with the tragedy?"

"Out through that window, three years ago to a day, her husband and her two young brothers went off for their day's shooting. They never came back. In crossing the moor to their favorite snipe-shooting ground, they were all three engulfed in a treacherous piece of bog. It had been that dreadful wet summer, you know, and places that were safe in other years gave way suddenly without warning. The bodies were never recovered. That was the dreadful part of it." Here the child's voice lost its self-possessed note and became falteringly human. "Poor aunt always thinks they will come back someday, they and the little brown spaniel that was lost with them, and walk in at that window just as they used to do. That is why the window is kept open every evening till it is quite dusk. Poor dear aunt, she has often told me how they went out, her husband with his white waterproof coat over his arm, and Ronnie, her youngest brother, singing 'Bertie, why do you bound?' as he always did to tease her. Do you know, sometimes on still, quiet evenings like this, I almost get a creepy feeling that they will all walk through that window—"

She broke off with a little shudder. It was a relief to Framton when the aunt bustled into the room with a whirl of apologies for being late in making her appearance. . . .

from **The Open Window**

28 Based on the context of paragraph 14, what does *bog* mean?

○ swamp

○ lake

○ seashore

○ cliff

29 According to the selection, why is Framton Nuttel visiting Mrs. Sappleton's house?

○ to ask for help with his medical problem

○ to find out what happened to her husband and brothers

○ to learn about the neighborhood

○ to meet people while he is staying in the country

30 What is the MOST LIKELY reason the author chose to use extensive dialogue in the story?

○ to make the story easier to write

○ to show the story is not serious

○ to create the opportunity to use dialects

○ to make the characters more real

from **The Open Window**

31 How does the flashback in the third paragraph contribute to the story?

○ It introduces an important character.

○ It provides background information.

○ It explains an important mystery.

○ It introduces a universal theme.

32 What is the theme of this passage?

33 How does this story reflect the cultural attitudes and beliefs of its author and the time period in which it was written?

34 How does the niece seem to feel about what has happened and the way that her aunt has dealt with it? Use her dialogue to support your response.

WRITING PROCESSES 1

Read the passage below. Then answer the following questions.

Things Aren't Always What They Seem

Two days ago, Ruth had received the call. Her article willl be
 1   2
in this Sunday's paper. An hour later, Ruth spoke to her parents.
                            3
"Mom, dad, I have something to tell you." Her heart beat fast.
   4   5

"What is it, dear?" her mother asked. She didn't like the sound of
      6   7
her daughter's voice. Ruth was nervous.
                        8

"I, um . . ." Ruth cleared her throat and ignored the drummer who'd
 9   10
moved from her chest into her stomack. "Just spit it out, Ruth." Her
                                        11   12
dad's voice had that hard edge it got when he was annoyed.

"And you'll be reading it, in tomorrow's paper."
 13

What followed was nothing short of an interogation as Ruth's
 14
parents drilled her with questions. Whatdid the article say? Why
                                     15   16
had she done this? Why hadn't she told them? Ruth squirmed as
                17   18
she tries to answer each as fast as possible.

When it was all over, Ruth felt more confused that ever. She'd
 19   20
expected the drill. She hadn't expected that her parents might actu-
                          21
ally be pleased.

143

Writing Processes 1

35 In sentence 10, which word is misspelled?

- ○ ignored
- ○ drummer
- ○ chest
- ○ stomack

36 In sentences 3 and 4, which word should be capitalized?

- ○ hour
- ○ parents
- ○ dad
- ○ you

37 In sentence 2, which is the correct form of the verb *will be*?

- ○ would be
- ○ was
- ○ were
- ○ will have been

38 Which of the following sentences has a punctuation error?

- ○ sentence 13
- ○ sentence 14
- ○ sentence 17
- ○ sentence 19

Writing Processes 1

39 Sentence 18 contains an error in tense. Rewrite the sentence so that the error is corrected.

_____
_____
_____
_____

WRITING PROCESSES 2

Read the passage below. Then answer the following questions.

The Peace Corps

Have you ever wanted to make an important contribution? Did
¹   ²
you ever think there is more to life than getting an ordinary job and
buying CD's and clothes? But didn't know how to do it. Well, since
                                             ³   ⁴
1961, over 125,000 people have made such a contribution.

In 1961 President John F. Kennedy started an organization it was
                                                                                                ⁵
called the Peace Corps. The goal of the organization was to help
                                           ⁶
the people in developing nations. When it was first started, college
                                                        ⁷
graduates were needed to work in the areas of education, agriculture, health, and engineering. The Peace Corps volunteers became
                                                                   ⁸
involved in many kinds of projects. Today, volunteers from a great
                                                                         ⁹
number of fields are welcomed into the Peace Corps.

What happens when a person volunteer to join the Peace Corps?
                                                        ¹⁰
People of all ages can join. First, you must fill out forms about your
¹¹   ¹²
background. And why you wish to be a Peace Corps volunteer.
                   ¹³

Then you will be called for an interview if your skills match the
              ¹⁴
needs of the organization. Peace Corps volunteers may go to Africa,
                                                                      ¹⁵
Asia, Latin America, Eastern Europe, and the former Soviet Union.

Writing Processes 2

40 Which of the following sentences is a sentence fragment?

○ sentence 1

○ sentence 3

○ sentence 6

○ sentence 11

41 In sentence 2, what is wrong with the word CD's?

○ Only the C should be capitalized.

○ Neither letter should not be capitalized.

○ It should not have an apostrophe.

○ It should be spelled "CDes."

42 Which of the following sentences are sentences that should be combined?

○ sentence 1 and 2

○ sentence 5 and 6

○ sentence 7 and 8

○ sentence 12 and 13

43 In sentence 10, which is the correct form of the word *volunteer*?

○ volunteers

○ volunteered

○ will volunteer

○ no error

Writing Processes 2

44 Sentence 5 is a run-on sentence. Rewrite it so that it reads smoothly.

_____
_____
_____
_____

WRITING PROMPT

Plan, write, and proofread a narrative in response to the writing prompt below. Write your narrrative on your own paper.

> There are those who believe that lessons can be learned in all aspects of one's life. Write a narrative about an event in your life that taught you a lesson. Write about what happened in detail, following a logical order. Then explain what lesson you learned.

As you write your narrative, remember to
- Write a narrative, or story.
- Include details about the setting, people, and events.
- Use dialogue for the words that you and others say.
- Clearly explain the lesson that you learned.
- Edit your narrative for standard grammar, usage, spelling, and punctuation.

Writing Conventions

Read each question and choose the BEST answer.

45 Choose the answer that shows the CORRECT spelling of all words.

○ Ella watered the plants and straitened the magazines before she left for rehearsal this morning.

○ Ella watered the plants and straightened the magazines before she left for rehearsal this morning.

○ Ella watered the plants and straightened the magazines before she left for rehersal this morning.

○ Ella watered the plants and straightened the magasines before she left for rehearsal this morning.

46 Choose the answer that shows the CORRECT capitalization.

○ The title of Daryl's paper was *The sunniest little town in the sunshine state.*

○ The title of Daryl's paper was *The Sunniest Little Town In The Sunshine State.*

○ The title of Daryl's paper was *The sunniest little town in the Sunshine State.*

○ The title of Daryl's paper was *The Sunniest Little Town in the Sunshine State.*

47 Choose the answer that shows the CORRECT punctuation.

○ To get in shape, Dino has been running, lifting weights, and swimming.

○ To get in shape Dino has been running, lifting weights, and swimming.

○ To get in shape, Dino has been running lifting weights and swimming.

○ To get in shape Dino has been running lifting weights and swimming.

48 Choose the sentence that is written with the CORRECT capitalization and punctuation.

○ Before becoming president of the U.S. in 1913, Woodrow Wilson was governor of New Jersey.

○ Before becoming President of the U.S. in 1913, Woodrow Wilson was governor of New Jersey.

○ Before becoming President of the U.S. in, 1913, Woodrow Wilson was Governor of New Jersey.

○ Before becoming president of the US in 1913, Woodrow Wilson was governor of New Jersey.

49 Find the sentence that is complete and is written correctly.

○ Angela's friends were standing near the car on Saturday.

○ Angela's friends near the car on Saturday.

○ Were standing near the car on Saturday.

○ Angela and her friends all four near the car on Saturday morning.

50 Choose the word or words that BEST complete the sentence.

The lawn needs _____ .

○ mowed

○ be mowed

○ to be mowed

○ be mowing

51 Choose the word that BEST completes the sentence.

Jenna feels _____ to have a large family.

- ○ luck
- ○ luckily
- ○ lucks
- ○ lucky

52 Read the sentence.

Neil is _____ about having meatloaf for dinner.

Which of these words means *to have a mix of positive and negative feelings*?

- ○ excited
- ○ angry
- ○ petulant
- ○ ambivalent

53 Read these sentences.

Ada rode a _____ horse every day for a week.
The car was _____ from side to side as it went down the road.

Choose the word that best completes BOTH sentences.

- ○ new
- ○ weaving
- ○ rocking
- ○ large

54 Read these sentences.

He showed _____ in joining the club.
I made $15.00 in _____ last month.

Choose the word that best completes BOTH sentences.

○ dividends

○ independence

○ reasons

○ interest

55 Choose the words that BEST complete the sentence.

Yesterday, five of the _____ the salt lick.

○ deer visited

○ deers visited

○ deer visit

○ deers visit

56 Read this sentence.

If it rains tomorrow let's go bowling.

If you were editing, what would be the MOST important thing to change?

○ Spell tomorrow differently.

○ Add an adverb or adjective.

○ Remove the apostrophe in let's.

○ Add a comma after tomorrow.

57 Read this sentence.

Minnie is 5'2" tall has long hair and weighs about 110 lbs.

If you were editing, what would be the MOST important thing to change?

○ Change <u>weighs</u> to <u>ways</u>.

○ Spell out the numbers.

○ Chang <u>lbs</u> to <u>pounds</u>.

○ Use commas to create a series.

58 Read this sentence.

Kanishas bright red shoes made her banana-yellow pants look even more flamboyant than I remembered.

If you were editing, what would be the MOST important thing to change?

○ Spell <u>flamboyant</u> differently.

○ Change the verb <u>made</u> to a more colorful word.

○ Take the hyphen out of "banana-yellow."

○ Change "Kanishas" to "Kanisha's."

59 Read this sentence.

Either Paul or Andrew will drop off _____ notes by 4:00.

Based on the antecedent, identify the pronoun that belongs in the blank.

○ his

○ their

○ its

○ they

60 Read this paragraph.

(1) The balls are kept in the large brown box to the left of the playground door. (2) Four-square is an old playground game with simple rules. (3) Begin by using chalk or duct tape to make a 2 x 2 grid on cement. (4) One player stands in each square of the grid. (5) The ball is bounced back and fourth between players and cannot be hit out of bounds, caught, nor bounced twice without being touched.

Choose the sentence that does not belong in the paragraph.

○ Sentence 1

○ Sentence 2

○ Sentence 4

○ Sentence 5

61 Read the paragraph. Then choose the BEST topic sentence for the paragraph.

_____ . The little town in southwest Maine has a population just under 2200 people. Twelve ponds and lakes exist around and in the town. Simple math clarifies that there is one lake or pond for every 180 people. Given that people are busy with many activities, it is reasonable to think that, on any given day, only 10 or 20 people would have to share any given body of water. Since these 10 or 20 people could spread out over the entire body of water, there really isn't a big need for sharing water space in Acton, Maine.

○ Acton, Maine, is not very far from Massachusetts.

○ Acton, Maine is a great place to live if you like to swim.

○ Everyone in Acton, Maine, owns at least one boat.

○ Water enthusiasts in Acton, Maine, don't have to learn to share.

Read this paragraph.

(1) The well pump was new to Andrea. (2) At her house, they had an outside water source, but it was just a faucet on the side of the house. (3) She was excited as she reached for the large curved handle that was curved to see if she could actually get some water out by pumping. (4) Andrea started raising the heavy handle with all her might, but she was caught of guard when it suddenly sprang a few inches on its own. (5) With blood running down her face, she went running to the house for some sympathy and ice.

62 Choose the sentence from the paragraph above that would be the BEST candidate for rewriting.

○ Sentence 2

○ Sentence 3

○ Sentence 4

○ Sentence 5

For Number 63, choose the underlined word that shows **improper grammar**.

63 My <u>sister</u> Wendy <u>are</u> going to <u>the</u> grocery store <u>now</u>.
     ○   ○   ○   ○

For Number 64, choose the underlined word that shows **improper grammar**.

64 If <u>you</u> <u>ask</u> a typical student, <u>they</u> will say that the red and yellow
   ○ ○   ○

combination <u>is</u> best.
            ○

Copyright © by Holt, Rinehart and Winston. All rights reserved.

For Number 65, choose the underlined word that shows **improper grammar**.

65 If you <u>sit</u> with Mark and <u>I</u>, you <u>will have</u> a <u>good</u> view.

      ○   ○   ○   ○

66 Choose the sentence that would be BEST removed from the paragraph.

(1) If you think about it, you will realize that chair seats are made of many different materials. (2) The most typical material is perhaps wood, but wood is not practical in every situation. (3) For one thing, indoor chairs and outdoor chairs are usually not alike. (4) For example, chairs that sit on porches, decks, or yards often have plastic straps, canvas, metal, wicker, plastic, rough wood, or stone seats. (5) On the other hand, chairs with finished wood, leather, and stuffed fabric seats are rarely used out of doors.

○ Sentence 2

○ Sentence 3

○ Sentence 4

○ Sentence 5

67 Choose the BEST way to combine these two sentences.

I like mixed nuts, because I really like walnuts, cashews, and pecans.

I don't want any peanuts in my mixed nuts.

○ I like mixed nuts, because I really like walnuts, cashews, and pecans, and I like them without peanuts.

○ I like mixed nuts without peanuts.

○ I like mixed nuts, because I really like walnuts, cashews, and pecans without peanuts.

○ I like mixed nuts without peanuts, because I really like walnuts, cashews, and pecans.

68 Choose the sentence that is written correctly.

○ Southeast Iowa's Lake Geode incorporates 187 acres, has a ramp for launching boats, and offers picnicking facilities.

○ Southeast Iowa's Lake Geode incourporates 187 acres, has a ramp for launching boats, and offers picnicing facilities.

○ Southeast Iowa's Lake Geode incorporates 187 acers, has a ramp for launching boats, and offers picnicking facilities.

○ Southeast Iowa's Lake Geode incorporates 187 acres, has a ramp for lawnching boats, and offers picnicking facilities.

69 Choose the sentence that BEST fills the blank in the paragraph.

If you want to buy a parrot and teach it to talk, the first step is to buy the right parrot. As a rule, parrot species that are smaller in size do not learn to talk as easily and do not talk as clearly as do larger parrots. If you are set on buying smaller parrot, the best way to find one that is likely to be a better-than-expected talker is to hang around a pet shop and listen. _____ . But, if you really want a talker, forget about the little parrots.

○ Most shop owners won't mind if you spend quite a bit of time with the parrots.

○ You will hear a lot of other animals, too, but you will probably be able to pick out the parrots.

○ The good talkers will pick up your name just from hearing the store clerk talk to you.

○ Those that are doing the most jabbering are your best bets.

Read the paragraph below to answer Number 70.

> **Some small parrots are good talkers and some large parrots are poor talkers. But, typically, the larger parrots are the best talkers. So, if you want a parrot that looks fast and talks clearly, look at the bigger parrots. A good example is the African Gray parrot, which some parrot enthusiasts say is the best talker of all parrots. So, and then buy an African Gray parrot and get ready to start teaching, because they will be ready to learn since they are great talkers and some people think they are the best-talking parrots!**

70 What is the BEST way to write the last sentence in this paragraph?

○ So, buy an African Gray parrot and get ready to start teaching!

○ So, look for a bigger parrot since they are better talkers.

○ So, get an African Gray parrot and perhaps it can teach you to talk!

○ So, find a parrot bigger than the African Gray parrot since bigger parrots talk better.

71 For what reason might a bicycle company employee write a set of directions for assembling a bicycle?

○ to entertain

○ to inform

○ to persuade

○ to apologize

72 In which of these written pieces would it make the MOST sense to use third person?

○ directions for using a drill

○ an invitation to a party

○ a diary entry

○ a front-page newspaper article

Read the paragraph below to answer Number 73.

> This summer, the Dowlings found themselves throwing a garden party without intending to. One day, they noticed a few bees in the yard and shrugged it off as natural for summer. _____ . Mr. Dowling went a little closer—not too close—and he could see a beehive inside the plant. He called the local honey organization and arranged to put an end to the garden party by paying to have the bees relocated.

73 Choose the sentence that BEST fills the blank in the paragraph.

○ It was a warm day, so they decided to go to the beach and have a picnic and swim a little.

○ A couple of weeks later, they realized there were a lot of bees swarming about the pampas plant.

○ Had it been winter, they would have been upset and would have tried to do something about it.

○ The relocation process took over four hours, and the guy said they would probably have to requeen the bees.

74 Read these four sentences.

1. Clara does not know the write way to turn.
2. Did you haul the chair in their truck?
3. Were you at their house when it happened?
4. That is quite a feat you have accomplished.

In which sentence is a homophone used incorrectly?

○ Sentence 1

○ Sentence 2

○ Sentence 3

○ Sentence 4

Name _____ Class _____ Date _____ Score _____

ANSWER SHEET

READING TEST PRACTICE
Circle the correct answer.

The Railroad Excursion
1. A B C D
2. A B C D
3. A B C D
4. A B C D
5. A B C D
6. A B C D
7. A B C D
8. A B C D
9. A B C D
10. Use a separate sheet of paper to record your response.

A Country Cottage
1. A B C D
2. A B C D
3. A B C D
4. A B C D
5. A B C D
6. A B C D
7. A B C D
8. A B C D
9. Fill in the chart in the workbook.
10. Use a separate sheet of paper to record your response.

from **My Ántonia, Book I, Part VI**
1. A B C D
2. A B C D
3. A B C D
4. A B C D
5. A B C D
6. A B C D
7. A B C D
8. A B C D
9–10. Use a separate sheet of paper to record your response.

from **Three Soldiers**
1. A B C D
2. A B C D
3. A B C D
4. A B C D
5. A B C D
6. A B C D
7. A B C D
8. Fill in the chart in the workbook.
9–10. Use a separate sheet of paper to record your response.

Space Junk
1. A B C D
2. A B C D
3. A B C D
4. A B C D
5. A B C D
6. A B C D
7. A B C D
8. A B C D
9–10. Use a separate sheet of paper to record your response.

To a Locomotive In Winter
1. A B C D
2. A B C D
3. A B C D
4. A B C D
5. A B C D
6. A B C D
7. A B C D
8. A B C D
9. A B C D
10. Use a separate sheet of paper to record your response.

Pangaea
1. A B C D
2. A B C D
3. A B C D
4. A B C D
5. A B C D
6. A B C D
7. A B C D
8. A B C D
9. Use a separate sheet of paper to record your response.
10. Fill in the chart in the workbook.

Copyright © by Holt, Rinehart and Winston. All rights reserved.

Name _____ Class _____ Date _____ Score _____

ANSWER SHEET

READING TEST PRACTICE
Circle the correct answer.

From Dream to Disaster

1. A B C D
2. A B C D
3. A B C D
4. A B C D
5. A B C D
6. A B C D
7. A B C D
8. A B C D

9–10 Use a separate sheet of paper to record your response.

Dispersal and Propagation of Plants

1. A B C D
2. A B C D
3. A B C D
4. A B C D
5. A B C D
6. A B C D
7. A B C D
8. A B C D
9. A B C D

10. Use a separate sheet of paper to record your response.

Schoolwork Employment Agency

1. A B C D
2. A B C D
3. A B C D
4. A B C D
5. A B C D
6. A B C D
7. A B C D
8. A B C D

9–10. Use a separate sheet of paper to record your response.

Wanted: School Spirit

1. A B C D
2. A B C D
3. A B C D
4. A B C D
5. A B C D
6. A B C D
7. A B C D
8. A B C D
9. A B C D

10. Use a separate sheet of paper to record your response.

Editorial to the City

1. A B C D
2. A B C D
3. A B C D
4. A B C D
5. A B C D
6. A B C D
7. A B C D
8. A B C D
9. A B C D

10. Use a separate sheet of paper to record your response.

The Wind/The Wind Tapped Like a Tired Man

1. A B C D
2. A B C D
3. A B C D
4. A B C D
5. A B C D
6. A B C D
7. A B C D

8–10. Use a separate sheet of paper to record your response.

Copyright © by Holt, Rinehart and Winston. All rights reserved.

Name _____ Class _____ Date _____ Score _____

ANSWER SHEET

WRITING TEST PRACTICE: WRITING CONVENTIONS
Circle the correct answer.

Writing Conventions Practice 1

1. A B C D
2. A B C D
3. A B C D
4. A B C D
5. A B C D
6. Use a separate sheet of paper to record your response.

Writing Conventions Practice 2

1. A B C D
2. A B C D
3. A B C D
4. A B C D
5. A B C D
6. Use a separate sheet of paper to record your response.

Writing Conventions Practice 3

1. A B C D
2. A B C D
3. A B C D
4. A B C D
5. A B C D
6. Use a separate sheet of paper to record your response.

Writing Conventions Practice 4

1. A B C D
2. A B C D
3. A B C D
4. A B C D
5. A B C D
6. Use a separate sheet of paper to record your response.

Writing Conventions Practice 5

1. A B C D
2. A B C D
3. A B C D
4. A B C D
5. A B C D
6. A B C D
7. A B C D
8. A B C D
9. A B C D
10. A B C D
11. A B C D
12. A B C D
13. A B C D
14. A B C D
15. A B C D